ASPEN PUBLISHE

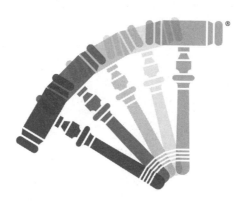

Casenote™ Legal Briefs

CONFLICTS

Keyed to Courses Using

Currie, Kay, Kramer, and Roosevelt

Conflict of Laws

Eighth Edition

Wolters Kluwer

Law & Business

AUSTIN   BOSTON   CHICAGO   NEW YORK   THE NETHERLANDS

This publication is designed to provide accurate and authoritative information in regard to the subject matter covered. It is sold with the understanding that the publisher is not engaged in rendering legal, accounting, or other professional services. If legal advice or other expert assistance is required, the services of a competent professional person should be sought.

> — From a Declaration of Principles adopted jointly by a Committee of the American Bar Association and a Committee of Publishers and Associates

To contact Customer Care, e-mail customer.service@aspenpublishers.com, call 1-800-234-1660, fax 1-800-901-9075, or mail correspondence to:

Aspen Publishers
Attn: Order Department
P.O. Box 990
Frederick, MD 21705

Printed in the United States of America.

1 2 3 4 5 6 7 8 9 0

ISBN 978-0-7355-9904-8

About Wolters Kluwer Law & Business

Wolters Kluwer Law & Business is a leading provider of research information and workflow solutions in key specialty areas. The strengths of the individual brands of Aspen Publishers, CCH, Kluwer Law International and Loislaw are aligned within Wolters Kluwer Law & Business to provide comprehensive, in-depth solutions and expert-authored content for the legal, professional and education markets.

CCH was founded in 1913 and has served more than four generations of business professionals and their clients. The CCH products in the Wolters Kluwer Law & Business group are highly regarded electronic and print resources for legal, securities, antitrust and trade regulation, government contracting, banking, pension, payroll, employment and labor, and health-care reimbursement and compliance professionals.

Aspen Publishers is a leading information provider for attorneys, business professionals and law students. Written by preeminent authorities, Aspen products offer analytical and practical information in a range of specialty practice areas from securities law and intellectual property to mergers and acquisitions and pension/benefits. Aspen's trusted legal education resources provide professors and students with high-quality, up-to-date and effective resources for successful instruction and study in all areas of the law.

Kluwer Law International supplies the global business community with comprehensive English-language international legal information. Legal practitioners, corporate counsel and business executives around the world rely on the Kluwer Law International journals, loose-leafs, books and electronic products for authoritative information in many areas of international legal practice.

Loislaw is a premier provider of digitized legal content to small law firm practitioners of various specializations. Loislaw provides attorneys with the ability to quickly and efficiently find the necessary legal information they need, when and where they need it, by facilitating access to primary law as well as state-specific law, records, forms and treatises.

Wolters Kluwer Law & Business, a unit of Wolters Kluwer, is headquartered in New York and Riverwoods, Illinois. Wolters Kluwer is a leading multinational publisher and information services company.

Format for the Casenote Legal Brief

Nature of Case: This section identifies the form of action (e.g., breach of contract, negligence, battery), the type of proceeding (e.g., demurrer, appeal from trial court's jury instructions),or the relief sought (e.g., damages, injunction, criminal sanctions).

Fact Summary: This is included to refresh your memory and can be used as a quick reminder of the facts.

Rule of Law: Summarizes the general principle of law that the case illustrates. It may be used for instant recall of the court's holding and for classroom discussion or home review.

Facts: This section contains all relevant facts of the case, including the contentions of the parties and the lower court holdings. It is written in a logical order to give the student a clear understanding of the case. The plaintiff and defendant are identified by their proper names throughout and are always labeled with a (P) or (D).

Palsgraf v. Long Island R.R. Co.

Injured bystander (P) v. Railroad company (D)

N.Y. Ct. App., 248 N.Y. 339, 162 N.E. 99 (1928).

NATURE OF CASE: Appeal from judgment affirming verdict for plaintiff seeking damages for personal injury.

FACT SUMMARY: Helen Palsgraf (P) was injured on R.R.'s (D) train platform when R.R.'s (D) guard helped a passenger aboard a moving train, causing his package to fall on the tracks. The package contained fireworks which exploded, creating a shock that tipped a scale onto Palsgraf (P).

🏛 RULE OF LAW
The risk reasonably to be perceived defines the duty to be obeyed.

FACTS: Helen Palsgraf (P) purchased a ticket to Rockaway Beach from R.R. (D) and was waiting on the train platform. As she waited, two men ran to catch a train that was pulling out from the platform. The first man jumped aboard, but the second man, who appeared as if he might fall, was helped aboard by the guard on the train who had kept the door open so they could jump aboard. A guard on the platform also helped by pushing him onto the train. The man was carrying a package wrapped in newspaper. In the process, the man dropped his package, which fell on the tracks. The package contained fireworks and exploded. The shock of the explosion was apparently of great enough strength to tip over some scales at the other end of the platform, which fell on Palsgraf (P) and injured her. A jury awarded her damages, and R.R. (D) appealed.

ISSUE: Does the risk reasonably to be perceived define the duty to be obeyed?

HOLDING AND DECISION: (Cardozo, C.J.) Yes. The risk reasonably to be perceived defines the duty to be obeyed. If there is no foreseeable hazard to the injured party as the result of a seemingly innocent act, the act does not become a tort because it happened to be a wrong as to another. If the wrong was not willful, the plaintiff must show that the act as to her had such great and apparent possibilities of danger as to entitle her to protection. Negligence in the abstract is not enough upon which to base liability. Negligence is a relative concept, evolving out of the common law doctrine of trespass on the case. To establish liability, the defendant must owe a legal duty of reasonable care to the injured party. A cause of action in tort will lie where harm,

though unintended, could have been averted or avoided by observance of such a duty. The scope of the duty is limited by the range of danger that a reasonable person could foresee. In this case, there was nothing to suggest from the appearance of the parcel or otherwise that the parcel contained fireworks. The guard could not reasonably have had any warning of a threat to Palsgraf (P), and R.R. (D) therefore cannot be held liable. Judgment is reversed in favor of R.R. (D).

DISSENT: (Andrews, J.) The concept that there is no negligence unless R.R. (D) owes a legal duty to take care as to Palsgraf (P) herself is too narrow. Everyone owes to the world at large the duty of refraining from those acts that may unreasonably threaten the safety of others. If the guard's action was negligent as to those nearby, it was also negligent as to those outside what might be termed the "danger zone." For Palsgraf (P) to recover, R.R.'s (D) negligence must have been the proximate cause of her injury, a question of fact for the jury.

▶ ANALYSIS
The majority defined the limit of the defendant's liability in terms of the danger that a reasonable person in defendant's situation would have perceived. The dissent argued that the limitation should not be placed on liability, but rather on damages. Judge Andrews suggested that only injuries that would not have happened but for R.R.'s (D) negligence should be compensable. Both the majority and dissent recognized the policy-driven need to limit liability for negligent acts, seeking, in the words of Judge Andrews, to define a framework "that will be practical and in keeping with the general understanding of mankind." The Restatement (Second) of Torts has accepted Judge Cardozo's view.

▬

Quicknotes
FORESEEABILITY A reasonable expectation that change is the probable result of certain acts or omissions.

NEGLIGENCE Conduct falling below the standard of care that a reasonable person would demonstrate under similar conditions.

PROXIMATE CAUSE The natural sequence of events without which an injury would not have been sustained.

▬

Party ID: Quick identification of the relationship between the parties.

Concurrence/Dissent: All concurrences and dissents are briefed whenever they are included by the casebook editor.

Analysis: This last paragraph gives you a broad understanding of where the case "fits in" with other cases in the section of the book and with the entire course. It is a hornbook-style discussion indicating whether the case is a majority or minority opinion and comparing the principal case with other cases in the casebook. It may also provide analysis from restatements, uniform codes, and law review articles. The analysis will prove to be invaluable to classroom discussion.

Issue: The issue is a concise question that brings out the essence of the opinion as it relates to the section of the casebook in which the case appears. Both substantive and procedural issues are included if relevant to the decision.

Holding and Decision: This section offers a clear and in-depth discussion of the rule of the case and the court's rationale. It is written in easy-to-understand language and answers the issue presented by applying the law to the facts of the case. When relevant, it includes a thorough discussion of the exceptions to the case as listed by the court, any major cites to the other cases on point, and the names of the judges who wrote the decisions.

Quicknotes: Conveniently defines legal terms found in the case and summarizes the nature of any statutes, codes, or rules referred to in the text.

Aspen Publishers is proud to offer *Casenote Legal Briefs*—continuing thirty years of publishing America's best-selling legal briefs.

Casenote Legal Briefs are designed to help you save time when briefing assigned cases. Organized under convenient headings, they show you how to abstract the basic facts and holdings from the text of the actual opinions handed down by the courts. Used as part of a rigorous study regimen, they can help you spend more time analyzing and critiquing points of law than on copying bits and pieces of judicial opinions into your notebook or outline.

Casenote Legal Briefs should never be used as a substitute for assigned casebook readings. They work best when read as a follow-up to reviewing the underlying opinions themselves. Students who try to avoid reading and digesting the judicial opinions in their casebooks or online sources will end up shortchanging themselves in the long run. The ability to absorb, critique, and restate the dynamic and complex elements of case law decisions is crucial to your success in law school and beyond. It cannot be developed vicariously.

Casenote Legal Briefs represents but one of the many offerings in Aspen's Study Aid Timeline, which includes:

- *Casenote Legal Briefs*
- *Emanuel Law Outlines*
- *Examples & Explanations* Series
- *Introduction to Law* Series
- Emanuel *Law in a Flash* Flash Cards
- Emanuel *CrunchTime* Series

Each of these series is designed to provide you with easy-to-understand explanations of complex points of law. Each volume offers guidance on the principles of legal analysis and, consulted regularly, will hone your ability to spot relevant issues. We have titles that will help you prepare for class, prepare for your exams, and enhance your general comprehension of the law along the way.

To find out more about Aspen Study Aid publications, visit us online at *www.AspenLaw.com* or email us at *legaledu@wolterskluwer.com*. We'll be happy to assist you.

Get this Casenote Legal Brief as an AspenLaw Studydesk eBook today!

By returning this form to Aspen Publishers, you will receive a complimentary eBook download of this Casenote Legal Brief and AspenLaw Studydesk productivity software.* Learn more about AspenLaw Studydesk today at *www.AspenLaw.com/Studydesk.*

Name	Phone ( )
Address	**Apt. No.**
City	**State**	**ZIP Code**
Law School	**Graduation Date** Month _____ Year _____

Cut out the UPC found on the lower left corner of the back cover of this book. Staple the UPC inside this box. Only the original UPC from the book cover will be accepted. (No photocopies or store stickers are allowed.)

Attach UPC inside this box.

Email (Print legibly or you may not get access!)
Title of this book (course subject)
ISBN of this book (10- or 13-digit number on the UPC)
Used with which casebook (provide author's name)

Mail the completed form to:
Aspen Publishers, Inc.
Legal Education Division
130 Turner Street, Bldg 3, 4th Floor
Waltham, MA 02453-8901

* Upon receipt of this completed form, you will be emailed a code for the digital download of this book in AspenLaw Studydesk eBook format and a free copy of the software application, which is required to read the eBook.

For a full list of eBook study aids available for AspenLaw Studydesk software and other resources that will help you with your law school studies, visit *www.AspenLaw.com.*

Make a photocopy of this form and your UPC for your records.

For detailed information on the use of the information you provide on this form, please see the PRIVACY POLICY at *www.AspenLaw.com.*

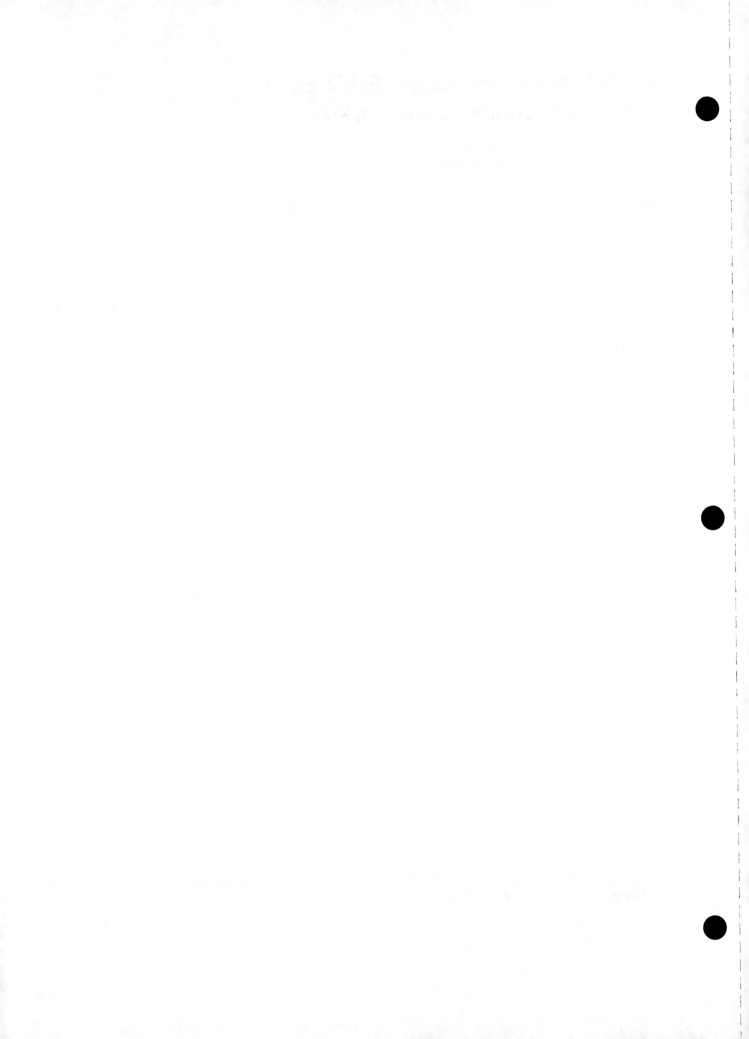

A. Decide on a Format and Stick to It

Structure is essential to a good brief. It enables you to arrange systematically the related parts that are scattered throughout most cases, thus making manageable and understandable what might otherwise seem to be an endless and unfathomable sea of information. There are, of course, an unlimited number of formats that can be utilized. However, it is best to find one that suits your needs and stick to it. Consistency breeds both efficiency and the security that when called upon you will know where to look in your brief for the information you are asked to give.

Any format, as long as it presents the essential elements of a case in an organized fashion, can be used. Experience, however, has led *Casenotes* to develop and utilize the following format because of its logical flow and universal applicability.

NATURE OF CASE: This is a brief statement of the legal character and procedural status of the case (e.g., "Appeal of a burglary conviction").

There are many different alternatives open to a litigant dissatisfied with a court ruling. The key to determining which one has been used is to discover *who is asking this court for what.*

This first entry in the brief should be kept as *short as possible.* Use the court's terminology if you understand it. But since jurisdictions vary as to the titles of pleadings, the best entry is the one that addresses who wants what in this proceeding, not the one that sounds most like the court's language.

RULE OF LAW: A statement of the general principle of law that the case illustrates (e.g., "An acceptance that varies any term of the offer is considered a rejection and counteroffer").

Determining the rule of law of a case is a procedure similar to determining the issue of the case. Avoid being fooled by red herrings; there may be a few rules of law mentioned in the case excerpt, but usually only one is *the* rule with which the casebook editor is concerned. The techniques used to locate the issue, described below, may also be utilized to find the rule of law. Generally, your best guide is simply the chapter heading. It is a clue to the point the casebook editor seeks to make and should be kept in mind when reading every case in the respective section.

FACTS: A synopsis of only the essential facts of the case, i.e., those bearing upon or leading up to the issue.

The facts entry should be a short statement of the events and transactions that led one party to initiate legal proceedings against another in the first place. While some cases conveniently state the salient facts at the beginning of the decision, in other instances they will have to be culled from hiding places throughout the text, even from concurring and dissenting opinions. Some of the "facts" will often be in dispute and should be so noted. Conflicting evidence may be briefly pointed up. "Hard" facts must be included. Both must be *relevant* in order to be listed in the facts entry. It is impossible to tell what is relevant until the entire case is read, as the ultimate determination of the rights and liabilities of the parties may turn on something buried deep in the opinion.

Generally, the facts entry should not be longer than three to five *short* sentences.

It is often helpful to identify the role played by a party in a given context. For example, in a construction contract case the identification of a party as the "contractor" or "builder" alleviates the need to tell that that party was the one who was supposed to have built the house.

It is always helpful, and a good general practice, to identify the "plaintiff" and the "defendant." This may seem elementary and uncomplicated, but, especially in view of the creative editing practiced by some casebook editors, it is sometimes a difficult or even impossible task. Bear in mind that the *party presently* seeking something from this court may not be the plaintiff, and that sometimes only the cross-claim of a defendant is treated in the excerpt. Confusing or misaligning the parties can ruin your analysis and understanding of the case.

ISSUE: A statement of the general legal question answered by or illustrated in the case. For clarity, the issue is best put in the form of a question capable of a "yes" or "no" answer. In reality, the issue is simply the Rule of Law put in the form of a question (e.g., "May an offer be accepted by performance?").

The major problem presented in discerning what is *the* issue in the case is that an opinion usually purports to raise and answer several questions. However, except for rare cases, only one such question is really the issue in the case. Collateral issues not necessary to the resolution of the matter in controversy are handled by the court by language known as *"obiter dictum"* or merely *"dictum."* While dicta may be included later in the brief, they have no place under the issue heading.

To find the issue, ask *who wants what* and then go on to ask *why did that party succeed or fail in getting it.* Once this is determined, the "why" should be turned into a question.

The complexity of the issues in the cases will vary, but in all cases a single-sentence question should sum up the issue. *In a few cases,* there will be two, or even more rarely, three issues of equal importance to the resolution of the case. Each should be expressed in a single-sentence question.

Since many issues are resolved by a court in coming to a final disposition of a case, the casebook editor will reproduce the portion of the opinion containing the issue or issues most relevant to the area of law under scrutiny. A noted law professor gave this advice: "Close the book; look at the title on the cover." Chances are, if it is Property, you need not concern yourself with whether, for example, the federal government's treatment of the plaintiff's land really raises a federal question sufficient to support jurisdiction on this ground in federal court.

The same rule applies to chapter headings designating sub-areas within the subjects. They tip you off as to what the text is designed to teach. The cases are arranged in a casebook to show a progression or development of the law, so that the preceding cases may also help.

It is also most important to remember to *read the notes and questions* at the end of a case to determine what the editors wanted you to have gleaned from it.

HOLDING AND DECISION: This section should succinctly explain the rationale of the court in arriving at its decision. In capsulizing the "reasoning" of the court, it should always include an application of the general rule or rules of law to the specific facts of the case. Hidden justifications come to light in this entry: the reasons for the state of the law, the public policies, the biases and prejudices, those considerations that influence the justices' thinking and, ultimately, the outcome of the case. At the end, there should be a short indication of the disposition or procedural resolution of the case (e.g., "Decision of the trial court for Mr. Smith (P) reversed").

The foregoing format is designed to help you "digest" the reams of case material with which you will be faced in your law school career. Once mastered by practice, it will place at your fingertips the information the authors of your casebooks have sought to impart to you in case-by-case illustration and analysis.

B. Be as Economical as Possible in Briefing Cases

Once armed with a format that encourages succinctness, it is as important to be economical with regard to the time spent on the actual reading of the case as it is to be economical in the writing of the brief itself. This does not mean "skimming" a case. Rather, it means reading the case with an "eye" trained to recognize into which "section" of your brief a particular passage or line fits and having a system for quickly and precisely marking the case so that the passages fitting any one particular part of

the brief can be easily identified and brought together in a concise and accurate manner when the brief is actually written.

It is of no use to simply repeat everything in the opinion of the court; record only enough information to trigger your recollection of what the court said. Nevertheless, an accurate statement of the "law of the case," i.e., the legal principle applied to the facts, is absolutely essential to class preparation and to learning the law under the case method.

To that end, it is important to develop a "shorthand" that you can use to make marginal notations. These notations will tell you at a glance in which section of the brief you will be placing that particular passage or portion of the opinion.

Some students prefer to underline all the salient portions of the opinion (with a pencil or colored underliner marker), making marginal notations as they go along. Others prefer the color-coded method of underlining, utilizing different colors of markers to underline the salient portions of the case, each separate color being used to represent a different section of the brief. For example, blue underlining could be used for passages relating to the rule of law, yellow for those relating to the issue, and green for those relating to the holding and decision, etc. While it has its advocates, the color-coded method can be confusing and time-consuming (all that time spent on changing colored markers). Furthermore, it can interfere with the continuity and concentration many students deem essential to the reading of a case for maximum comprehension. In the end, however, it is a matter of personal preference and style. Just remember, whatever method you use, underlining must be used sparingly or its value is lost.

If you take the marginal notation route, an efficient and easy method is to go along underlining the key portions of the case and placing in the margin alongside them the following "markers" to indicate where a particular passage or line "belongs" in the brief you will write:

N   (NATURE OF CASE)
RL   (RULE OF LAW)
I   (ISSUE)
HL   (HOLDING AND DECISION, relates to
      the RULE OF LAW behind the decision)
HR   (HOLDING AND DECISION, gives the
      RATIONALE or reasoning behind the
      decision)
HA   (HOLDING AND DECISION, APPLIES
      the general principle(s) of law to the facts
      of the case to arrive at the decision)

Remember that a particular passage may well contain information necessary to more than one part of your brief, in which case you simply note that in the margin. If you are using the color-coded underlining method instead of marginal notation, simply make asterisks or checks in the margin next to the passage in question in the colors that indicate the additional sections of the brief where it might be utilized.

The economy of utilizing "shorthand" in marking cases for briefing can be maintained in the actual brief writing process itself by utilizing "law student shorthand" within the brief. There are many commonly used words and phrases for which abbreviations can be substituted in your briefs (and in your class notes also). You can develop abbreviations that are personal to you and which will save you a lot of time. A reference list of briefing abbreviations can be found on page xii of this book.

C. Use Both the Briefing Process and the Brief as a Learning Tool

Now that you have a format and the tools for briefing cases efficiently, the most important thing is to make the time spent in briefing profitable to you and to make the most advantageous use of the briefs you create. Of course, the briefs are invaluable for classroom reference when you are called upon to explain or analyze a particular case. However, they are also useful in reviewing for exams. A quick glance at the fact summary should bring the case to mind, and a rereading of the rule of law should enable you to go over the underlying legal concept in your mind, how it was applied in that particular case, and how it might apply in other factual settings.

As to the value to be derived from engaging in the briefing process itself, there is an immediate benefit that arises from being forced to sift through the essential facts and reasoning from the court's opinion and to succinctly express them in your own words in your brief. The process ensures that you understand the case and the point that it illustrates, and that means you will be ready to absorb further analysis and information brought forth in class. It also ensures you will have something to say when called upon in class. The briefing process helps develop a mental agility for getting to the *gist* of a case and for identifying, expounding on, and applying the legal concepts and issues found there. The briefing process is the mental process on which you must rely in taking law school examinations; it is also the mental process upon which a lawyer relies in serving his clients and in making his living.

Abbreviations for Briefs

acceptance	acp	offer	O
affirmed	aff	offeree	OE
answer	ans	offeror	OR
assumption of risk	a/r	ordinance	ord
attorney	atty	pain and suffering	p/s
beyond a reasonable doubt	b/r/d	parol evidence	p/e
bona fide purchaser	BFP	plaintiff	P
breach of contract	br/k	prima facie	p/f
cause of action	c/a	probable cause	p/c
common law	c/l	proximate cause	px/c
Constitution	Con	real property	r/p
constitutional	con	reasonable doubt	r/d
contract	K	reasonable man	r/m
contributory negligence	c/n	rebuttable presumption	rb/p
cross	x	remanded	rem
cross-complaint	x/c	res ipsa loquitur	RIL
cross-examination	x/ex	respondeat superior	r/s
cruel and unusual punishment	c/u/p	Restatement	RS
defendant	D	reversed	rev
dismissed	dis	Rule Against Perpetuities	RAP
double jeopardy	d/j	search and seizure	s/s
due process	d/p	search warrant	s/w
equal protection	e/p	self-defense	s/d
equity	eq	specific performance	s/p
evidence	ev	statute	S
exclude	exc	statute of frauds	S/F
exclusionary rule	exc/r	statute of limitations	S/L
felony	f/n	summary judgment	s/j
freedom of speech	f/s	tenancy at will	t/w
good faith	g/f	tenancy in common	t/c
habeas corpus	h/c	tenant	t
hearsay	hr	third party	TP
husband	H	third party beneficiary	TPB
injunction	inj	transferred intent	TI
in loco parentis	ILP	unconscionable	uncon
inter vivos	I/v	unconstitutional	unconst
joint tenancy	j/t	undue influence	u/e
judgment	judgt	Uniform Commercial Code	UCC
jurisdiction	jur	unilateral	uni
last clear chance	LCC	vendee	VE
long-arm statute	LAS	vendor	VR
majority view	maj	versus	v
meeting of minds	MOM	void for vagueness	VFV
minority view	min	weight of authority	w/a
Miranda rule	Mir/r	weight of the evidence	w/e
Miranda warnings	Mir/w	wife	W
negligence	neg	with	w/
notice	ntc	within	w/i
nuisance	nus	without	w/o
obligation	ob	without prejudice	w/o/p
obscene	obs	wrongful death	wr/d

Table of Cases

Choice of Law: Traditional Approach

Quick Reference Rules of Law

Alabama Great Southern R.R. Co. v. Carroll

Employer (D) v. Injured employee (P)

Ala. Sup. Ct., 97 Ala. 126, 11 So. 803 (1892).

NATURE OF CASE: Action in tort on a theory of negligence.

FACT SUMMARY: Carroll (P), a railroad brakeman, was injured in Mississippi as a result of his fellow employees' failure to inspect the brakes in Alabama.

🏛 RULE OF LAW
Where a negligent act is committed in one state, but causes injury in another, an action seeking damages for injuries sustained as a result of the act may be brought only in the state in which the result is manifested, and not where the act was committed.

FACTS: Carroll (P), a resident of Alabama, was injured in Mississippi due to a break in a defective railroad car link. The Railroad's (D) employees had been negligent in their duty to inspect the links in Alabama. Carroll (P) sued the Railroad (D) in Alabama under a state statute which authorized recovery. Mississippi, which had no similar statute, would have denied recovery.

ISSUE: May recovery for a tortious act be obtained in the state in which the breach of duty but not the injury occurred?

HOLDING AND DECISION: (McClellan, J.) No. The general rule is that there can be no recovery in one state for injuries to the person sustained in another state unless the infliction of the injuries is actionable under the law of the state in which they were received. Here, up to the time the train passed out of Alabama, no injury had resulted. The Alabama statute has no efficiency beyond state lines. Only Mississippi could exert proper jurisdiction over the claim. A different result might have obtained if Carroll (P) had been injured in Alabama but suffered in Mississippi. As for an argument that the Railroad (D) was under a contractual duty to Carroll (P) which arose in Alabama, the Alabama law will govern only the incidents of the employment relationship and not with any specific contractual obligations. Reversed and remanded.

▶ ANALYSIS

Under the First Restatement, where a tort is involved the choice of law focuses on the situs of the wrong—that is, where the last occurrence required to make the defendant liable has transpired. This will usually be the place of plaintiff's injury.

Quicknotes

NEGLIGENCE Conduct falling below the standard of care that a reasonable person would demonstrate under similar conditions.

SITUS Location; in community property, the location of an asset.

Milliken v. Pratt

Maine supplier (P) v. Massachusetts debtor (D)

Mass. Jud. Sup. Ct., 125 Mass. 374 (1878).

NATURE OF CASE: Suit to enforce payment by a guarantor.

FACT SUMMARY: Pratt (D), a Massachusetts resident, signed a guaranty for the benefit of her husband's creditor, Milliken (P), a Maine supplier. At the time of the signing, she was incapable, by Massachusetts law, of entering into such a contract although no such disability existed in Maine.

🏛 RULE OF LAW
A contract that is valid by the law of the state where it was made is enforceable everywhere including states where such contracts are statutorily invalid.

FACTS: Mr. Pratt, as a condition of buying on credit from Milliken (P), obtained a signed guaranty for his debts from his wife, Mrs. Pratt (D). At the time of the signing, Pratt (D) was a resident of Massachusetts and by the law of that state a married woman was statutorily incapable of acting as surety for her husband. The guaranty was mailed to Milliken (P) in Maine, his place of business, where he shipped goods in reliance thereon. Upon the subsequent default of her husband, Pratt (D) refused demand on the guaranty and Milliken (P) brought suit against her in Massachusetts. The court ordered judgment for Pratt (D). Milliken (P) appealed.

ISSUE: May a contract validly made in one state be enforceable against the citizens of another state in the courts of the second state where such contracts are statutorily invalid?

HOLDING AND DECISION: (Gray, C.J.) Yes. The validity of a contract is to be determined by the law of the state where it was made. If it was valid there, then it is valid and enforceable everywhere. If enforcement is sought in the courts of a state that holds such contracts invalid, it is still enforceable unless the contract is immoral in nature. The acceptance of this contract occurred in Maine when Milliken (P) acted on the guaranty. The sales occurred there, since delivery was made by common carrier paid for by Pratt (D). If the incapacity of a married woman were a universal and unchanging situation, then enforcement of this contract in Massachusetts might be denied. But the contractual capacity of women is constantly expanding and, in fact, Massachusetts has subsequently allowed married women to enter into such contracts. Therefore, the guaranty is properly enforceable in Massachusetts. Reversed.

▶ ANALYSIS

The traditional rules governing when a contract is formed have also been deemed to show where it was made. Since this contract was accepted by shipment, the place of shipment determined where the contract was made. The "vested rights" approach to contract led to strange results as where a Mississippi woman, with full rights to contracts, was allowed to void a purchase in Tennessee, since Tennessee did not recognize her contractual capacity.

Quicknotes

COMITY A rule pursuant to which courts in one state give deference to the statutes and judicial decisions of another.

GUARANTOR A party who agrees to be liable for the debt or default of another.

VESTED RIGHT Rights in pension or other retirement benefits that are attained when the employee satisfies the minimum requirements necessary in order to be entitled to the receipt of such benefits in the future.

In re Barrie's Estate

[Parties not identified.]

Iowa Sup. Ct., 240 Iowa 431, 35 N.W.2d 658 (1949).

NATURE OF CASE: Probate of a will.

FACT SUMMARY: Barrie's will devising real property in Iowa and personal property in Illinois was denied probate in Illinois, but Iowa held that under its laws the will was valid.

⬛ RULE OF LAW
The Full Faith and Credit Clause does not render foreign decrees of probate conclusive as to the validity of a will with respect to real property situated in a state other than the one in which the decree was rendered, nor do the doctrines of res judicata or collateral estoppel apply.

FACTS: Barrie died domiciled in Illinois owning real property in Iowa and personal property in Illinois. Her will directed that all her property be liquidated and then distributed in cash. The will was offered for probate in Illinois, but Illinois held that under its laws the testator had revoked the will and thus her property would go by the laws of intestate succession to her heirs at law. The beneficiary of the will offered it for probate in Iowa. Barrie's heirs at law asserted that the Illinois judgment was binding on the Iowa court. Under Iowa law, Barrie had not revoked the will, so the property would go to those named in this will and to the heirs at law.

ISSUE: Does the Full Faith and Credit Clause render foreign decrees of probate conclusive as to the validity of a will with respect to real property situated in a state other than the one in which the decree was rendered, and do the doctrines of res judicata or collateral estoppel apply?

HOLDING AND DECISION: (Hays, J.) No. The general rule is that the validity and effect of a will, including an intended revocation, by which real property is devised, is to be determined by the law of the state where the real property is located. The Full Faith and Credit Clause does not require the court of the state in which the land is located to treat foreign decrees which determine the validity of a will by which the land is devised as conclusive judgments. Also, the doctrines of res judicata and collateral estoppel do not apply to the findings of the first court. Title to real property can be determined only in the state in which the property is located. Iowa is free to place its own construction on the will of a nonresident of Iowa who dies owning real property situated in Iowa. This is true regardless of whether the will was admitted to probate in another state prior to the Iowa judgment. The Iowa statute will determine whether the will has been revoked, and so the Illinois judgment is not conclusive and binding on Iowa courts insofar as the disposition of real property in Iowa is concerned. Reversed and remanded.

▶ ANALYSIS

While the opinion in the dissent calling for a uniform law applying to all parts of an estate is appealing, one problem is presented by out-of-state wills operating on in-state property. Since the state where the land is located has ultimate control over the passage of title to such land, any out-of-state disposition of the property may impose an unreasonable burden on the ability of the forum state to keep a stable record of title. Where the forum controls disposition of all land within its borders, no such problem is presented. Questions of intestate succession to land; the validity, construction, revocation and effect of a will devising land; capacity to inherit land; and the rights of a surviving spouse in land are all governed by the law of the situs of the property. This includes the entire relevant law of the situs, including its conflicts law.

■■■

Quicknotes

COLLATERAL ESTOPPEL A doctrine whereby issues litigated and determined in a prior proceeding are binding upon all subsequent litigation between the parties regarding that issue.

FULL FAITH AND CREDIT Doctrine that a judgment by a court of one state shall be given the same effect in another state.

INTESTATE To die without leaving a valid testamentary instrument.

RES JUDICATA The rule of law that a final judgment by a court precludes subsequent litigation between the parties regarding the same cause of action.

■■■

White v. Tennant

Relatives (P) v. Administrator (D)

31 W.Va. 790, 8 S.E. 596 (1888).

NATURE OF CASE: Action to set aside settlement and distribution of an estate.

FACT SUMMARY: Michael White moved his home from West Virginia to Pennsylvania, but the same day crossed back to care for his wife who had typhoid. He caught the disease, died in West Virginia, and the question arose, for purposes of intestate succession, as to which state was his domicile.

⚖ RULE OF LAW

The law of the state in which the decedent had his domicile at the time of his death will control the succession and distribution of his personal estate.

FACTS: Michael White had his legal domicile in West Virginia, where he had lived all his life and owned a farm. Under an agreement he made with his mother, brothers and sisters, Michael sold his farm and was to occupy a house on 40 acres of land in Pennsylvania, just across the West Virginia state line. The acreage was part of a larger family farm on both sides of the state line with a mansion-house located on the West Virginia side. Michael and his wife arrived at their new home with their possessions and livestock. The house being cold and damp and his wife feeling ill, Michael accepted an invitation to spend the night in the West Virginia mansion-house. They left for the house after unloading their possessions. Michael's wife, it so happened, had typhoid fever. He cared for her at the mansion-house, going into Pennsylvania daily to care for his stock. Two weeks later, Michael came down with typhoid and died in West Virginia. His wife recovered and her father, Tennant (D), was appointed administrator of Michael's estate. Under West Virginia law, Michael's wife would receive all her husband's personal property by intestate succession. Under Pennsylvania law, she would receive only half, and his immediate family would get the other half. White (P), the brothers and sisters of Michael, sought to set aside the West Virginia distribution of his estate, claiming he was domiciled in Pennsylvania.

ISSUE: Will the law of the state in which the decedent had his domicile at the time of his death control the succession and distribution of his personal estate?

HOLDING AND DECISION: (Snyder, J.) Yes. The law of the state in which the decedent had his domicile at the time of death will control the succession and distribution of his personal estate. A domicile is a residence, actual or inchoate, with the lack of any intent to make a domicile elsewhere. These two elements must exist together. One domicile cannot be lost until another is acquired. From the facts, it appears that Michael abandoned his West Virginia residence with the intention and purpose not only of not returning to it, but for the expressed purpose of making a permanent home in Pennsylvania. Thus, at the instant he and his wife arrived at their new home, their domicile became Pennsylvania. His leaving there, under the circumstances, with the intention of returning there did not change that fact. He did not revive his West Virginia domicile because he had sold his residence and left it without any purpose of returning there. Accordingly, the decree must be reversed and remanded.

▶ *ANALYSIS*

The function of domicile is to enable the legal interests of a person to be determined by a single law "particularly in matters where continuity of application of the same law is important . . ." Under the Second Restatement of Conflicts, it is suggested that domicile will not attach until a person has been there for "a time," which is some time more than "a moment's presence." Note that should a husband send his wife on ahead to their new, intended domicile, her arrival there may be satisfactory to establish the husband's new domicile before his arrival.

Quicknotes

DOMICILE A person's permanent home or principal establishment to which he has an intention of returning when he is absent therefrom.

INTESTATE SUCCESSION The scheme pursuant to which property is distributed in the absence of a valid will or of a disposition of particular property.

Levy v. Daniels' U-Drive Auto Renting Co.

Injured passenger (P) v. Car rental company (D)

Conn. Sup. Ct., 108 Conn. 333, 143 A. 163 (1928).

NATURE OF CASE: Action for damages for negligence.

FACT SUMMARY: Levy (P), a passenger in an auto rented by Sack (D) from Daniels (D) in Connecticut, was injured when the auto was involved in an accident in Massachusetts, and he sued for damages in Connecticut.

🏛 RULE OF LAW
Liability arising out of a contract depends upon the law of the place of contract, unless the contract is to be performed or to have its beneficial operation and effect elsewhere, or it is made with reference to the law of another place.

FACTS: Daniels (D), an auto rental company located in Hartford, rented an auto to Sack (D). At the time of the events in question, Connecticut law provided that anyone who rents a motor vehicle to another shall be liable for any damage to any person or property caused by operation of the vehicle during the rental period. Levy (P) was a passenger in the rented auto when Sack (D) negligently drove on a Massachusetts highway where Maginn (D) negligently collided with Sack's (D) vehicle. Levy (P) suffered severe injuries as a result of their negligence and sued Daniels (D) in Connecticut, seeking to apply the Connecticut statute. Massachusetts had no statute defining the liability of renters of motor vehicles. Daniels (D) demurred, arguing that the law of the place of the tort should apply. Levy (P) claimed he was suing upon a contract. The demurrer was sustained.

ISSUE: Does the liability arising out of a contract depend upon the law of the place of contract, unless the contract is to be performed or to have its beneficial operation and effect elsewhere, or it is made with reference to the law of another place?

HOLDING AND DECISION: (Wheeler, C.J.) Yes. Liability arising out of a contract depends upon the law of the place of contract, unless the contract is to be performed or to have its beneficial operation and effect elsewhere, or is made with reference to the law of another place. The purpose of the Connecticut statute was to protect highway users by urging renters to make their vehicles available only to cautious and able drivers. The renter's liability was made a part of every contract for vehicle rental in Connecticut. The obligation imposed by law was for the direct, sole, and exclusive benefit of Levy (P). The contract was made for him and every other member of the public. Levy (P) was a beneficiary of the contract between Daniels (D) and Sack (D). Levy's (P) being injured determined his identity as a beneficiary and his right of action. While Levy's

(P) complaint alleges tortious operation of the auto, his right to sue arose upon the contract. The demurrer should have been overruled.

▶ ANALYSIS

Under the First Restatement of Conflicts, the "vested rights" approach to choice of law is followed. Usually, for contracts, the law of the place of the making is applied for formation and interpretation questions, while the law of the place of performance is applied for questions relating to performance and damages.

Quicknotes

BENEFICIARY A third party who is the recipient of the benefit of a transaction undertaken by another.

NEGLIGENCE Conduct falling below the standard of care that a reasonable person would demonstrate under similar conditions.

PUBLIC ACTS OF CONNECTICUT, § 21 Any person leasing a motor vehicle to another is liable for damages caused by operation of the leased vehicle.

VESTED RIGHT Rights in pension or other retirement benefits that are attained when the employee satisfies the minimum requirements necessary in order to be entitled to the receipt of such benefits in the future.

Haumschild v. Continental Casualty Co.

Injured passenger (P) v. Insurance company (D)

Wis. Sup. Ct., 7 Wis. 2d 130, 95 N.W.2d 814 (1959).

NATURE OF CASE: Suit in tort by wife against husband.

FACT SUMMARY: Mrs. Haumschild (P) was injured due to her husband's negligence while they were traveling in California. She brought suit in Wisconsin where they lived.

🏛 RULE OF LAW
Interspousal immunity for tort actions is a rule of family law and not tort law and the law of the spouses' domicile governs, not the law of the place of the wrong.

FACTS: Mrs. Haumschild (P) and her husband (D) were residents of Wisconsin traveling in California. While in California, Mrs. Haumschild (P) was injured due to her husband's (D) negligence in a car accident. California law prohibited a suit by a wife against her husband, or vice versa, for negligence. Wisconsin law contained no such prohibition. Suit was brought by Mrs. Haumschild (P) against her husband (D) in Wisconsin.

ISSUE: Where the place of the wrong prohibits interspousal suits for negligence, may the court of the spouses' domicile apply its own law which would allow such suits?

HOLDING AND DECISION: (Currie, J.) Yes. Where the place of the wrong prohibits interspousal suits for negligence, the court of the spouses' domicile may apply its own law which would allow such suits. The case presented is an issue of capacity to sue due to marital status. This relates to substantive family law and not to substantive tort law. While the majority of the states recognize the place of the wrong as governing capacity, we feel that the state of the domicile has a greater interest in such cases than the state where the wrong occurred. While California's conflict of laws rule would refer to our law to determine the wife's capacity, we do not feel it proper to resort to the awkward principles of renvoi to achieve what we feel to be the desired result. The law of the place of the wrong will govern as to substantive tort law, but the law of the domicile will govern as to capacity to sue. Mrs. Haumschild should be allowed to recover. Reversed and remanded.

▶ ANALYSIS

If the state of domicile will govern on the issue of interspousal immunity, then a California wife injured by her husband would be denied recovery in a Wisconsin court. But if the state of domicile views the immunity question as procedural tort law, the court's decision would appear unsatisfactory. Wisconsin would then be imposing its substantive family law as a substitute for the other state's procedural tort law. On balance, however, the Wisconsin court's approach would appear to be well-reasoned, since the marital partners' expectations (in a fictional sense) would appear to be grounded in the family law of their domicile.

■═■

Quicknotes

DOMICILE A person's permanent home or principal establishment to which he has an intention of returning when he is absent therefrom.

INTERSPOUSAL IMMUNITY A common law doctrine precluding spouses from commencing actions against one another for their torts.

RENVOI A doctrine pursuant to which a court adopts the conflict of law rules of a foreign jurisdiction, which requires the court to apply to the laws of its own forum.

■═■

Grant v. McAuliffe

Injured motorist (P) v. Estate administrator (D)

Cal. Sup. Ct., 41 Cal. 2d 859, 264 P.2d 944 (1953).

NATURE OF CASE: Suit for personal injuries brought by estate of deceased injured party.

FACT SUMMARY: Two California residents driving separate cars in Arizona collided with each other and one subsequently died. Under Arizona law, a tort action did not survive the death of the plaintiff, while under California law it did.

🏛 **RULE OF LAW**
Statutes which provide for the survival of a tort action if the plaintiff dies are procedural, not substantive, and may be applied to a suit arising out of an injury sustained in another jurisdiction.

FACTS: Pullen, a California resident and the driver of an automobile, died as the result of an auto accident in which he was the allegedly negligent party. The accident occurred in Arizona. Grant (P), also a California resident, was injured in the accident and sought damages from McAuliffe (D), Pullen's administrator. Under California law, tort actions survive the tortfeasor's death, while under Arizona law they do not. The California trial court found that Arizona law applied because it was of a substantive rather than procedural nature and, therefore, granted McAuliffe's (D) motion to abate Grant's (P) suit. Grant (P) appealed, arguing that the law was in fact procedural and thus the law of the forum, California, should apply.

ISSUE: Is a survival statute as to tort actions substantive law which would govern litigation over injuries sustained wherever the case is tried?

HOLDING AND DECISION: (Traynor, J.) No. A survival statute as to tort actions is not substantive law which would govern litigation over injuries sustained wherever the case is tried. This court recognizes the doctrine that the substantive law of the place of the wrong must govern litigation wherever it is tried. However, the forum state may always follow its own procedural rules of law. Finding the authorities split on whether a survival statute is procedural or substantive, this court will determine which argument is most meritorious. Since a survival statute does not create a new cause of action but merely allows the continuation of an existing action, it is procedural. All the relevant contacts are with California and the survival statute does not relate to liability but is a procedural rule to enforce claims for damages. Since a court may always follow its own procedural rules, this case may properly be tried under California law. Reversed and remanded.

DISSENT: (Schauer, J.) The characterization of this statute as procedural will produce a "rule" of law that is no rule at all. The only limit on the variable results this will produce is the limit of the judge's whimsy. Administration of an estate is a local procedure but the rights and liabilities of the parties in a personal injury suit are substantive.

▶ **ANALYSIS**

The California court was preparing the groundwork for abandoning the vested rights doctrine in choice of laws. The substance-procedure distinction was an escape device to allow the state which had the most contacts to apply its own law to the case. Arizona had no interest in this case, since all the parties and their families were in California.

◼━◼

Quicknotes

CALIFORNIA PROBATE CODE, § 573 Actions for physical injury or death may be maintained by or against estate administrators.

SURVIVAL STATUTE Law providing a cause of action to a deceased person's estate for certain unlawful acts committed upon the deceased person up until the time of his death.

VESTED RIGHT Rights in pension or other retirement benefits that are attained when the employee satisfies the minimum requirements necessary in order to be entitled to the receipt of such benefits in the future.

◼━◼

Bournias v. Atlantic Maritime Co., Ltd.

Employee (P) v. Employer (D)

220 F.2d 152 (2d Cir. 1955).

NATURE OF CASE: Suit under foreign labor code.

FACT SUMMARY: Bournias (P) brought suit under Panamanian law for back wages claimed to be due from Atlantic Maritime (D). Suit was brought in U.S. federal court beyond the Panamanian statutory limit.

RULE OF LAW

A statute of limitations is substantive, and therefore applicable in any forum, if it extinguishes the right sued upon and not the remedy.

FACTS: Bournias (P) was a seaman employed aboard a ship of Panamanian registry owned by Atlantic Maritime (D). He brought suit against Atlantic Maritime (D) for certain unpaid wage benefits claimed to be due him under the Panamanian labor code. The suit was instituted in U.S. federal court beyond the general statute of limitations providing for actions brought under the Panamanian code. Atlantic Maritime (D) moved to dismiss the suit as being barred by that statute of limitations.

ISSUE: Will a foreign statute of limitations be enforceable as substantive law in the forum if it extinguishes the right sued upon rather than merely barring the remedy?

HOLDING AND DECISION: (Harlan, J.) Yes. A forum called upon to enforce a right arising under foreign law is generally held to be privileged to apply its own rules of procedure to the case. In that view, statutes of limitation generally have been held to be procedural. An exception to this rule arises when the right sued upon is so interconnected with the limitation that the limitation is thought to extinguish the right rather than merely barring the remedy. Rather than attempting to ascertain if the foreign jurisdiction views its own statute of limitation as substantive or procedural or whether the forum would view it, in light of its own law, as substantive or procedural, a third more workable approach presents itself. The foreign substantive law to be enforced should be examined to see if there is a specific statute of limitations engrafted on the specific right sued upon or the statute of limitations is specifically pointed at the right sued upon. In the case before this court, the specific right sued upon is covered only by a general statute of limitations for the entire labor code. Certain specific rights within the code contain special limitations exempt from the general limitation. For that reason, this court finds that the limitation pertaining to the right sued upon here is procedural and not applicable in this court. The suit, being still maintainable under the forum statute of limitations, is not barred.

ANALYSIS

The Restatement (Second) on Conflicts holds that an action will not be maintained if it is not timely under the forum's law. It will be maintainable, if timely by the forum's law, even if it would be barred where the cause of action arose. There is one exception, in accord with the principal case, where the applicable foreign limitation bars the right and not merely the remedy.

Quicknotes

STATUTE OF LIMITATIONS A law prescribing the period in which a legal action may be commenced.

In re Schneider's Estate

Parties not identified.

N.Y. Surrogate Ct., 96 N.Y.S.2d 652, *adhered to on reargument*, 100 N.Y.S.2d 371 (1950).

NATURE OF CASE: Probate of a decedent's estate, including his will.

FACT SUMMARY: The decedent was a Swiss-born naturalized American, domiciled in New York. His will, which was probated in New York, contained a testamentary disposition of real property located in Switzerland that was impermissible under Swiss law.

🏛 RULE OF LAW
While the law of the situs of real property must control the disposition of that property, it is the whole law of the situs, including its conflict of laws rule, that must be applied.

FACTS: Schneider had been born in Switzerland but had come to the United States and had become a naturalized American citizen. He was domiciled in New York and died in that state. He left a will disposing of all of his assets. A portion of his assets disposed of by the will consisted of real property located in Switzerland in which he had retained ownership after his move to the United States. Internal Swiss law specified that certain portions of a decedent's property must descend to his legitimate heirs and that any testamentary disposition contrary to this law was void. The will was probated in New York. At the time of probate, the administratrix of the estate had liquidated the real property in Switzerland and had brought the funds so derived into New York. A claim was filed against the estate by the decedent's heirs in Switzerland claiming the right to the proceeds as determined by Swiss law. The testamentary disposition was valid under New York law.

ISSUE: Where the disposition of real property is to be determined by a court foreign to the situs of the property upon the death of the owner, must the forum court be bound by the local law of the situs without regard to the conflict of laws rule of the situs?

HOLDING AND DECISION: (Frankenthaler, Surrogate) No. First, the court qualified its jurisdiction over the claim by pointing out that the liquidation of the Swiss property and the transfer of the funds to New York effectively removed Swiss jurisdiction over the matter. However, the court determined that its decision must be made on the grounds that it was dealing with the real property and not the substituted fund. As such, the court recognized the universally accepted principle that the law of the situs of the real property can be the only law applied to controversies over disposition of that property. The New York court must, therefore, adjudicate the various claims relating to the Swiss property as though it were a Swiss court applying the whole law of Switzerland to the controversy. The conversion of the property to money and the relocation of that money to New York was held to be a fortuitous act of no consequence. But reference to the whole law of Switzerland would include a reference to the conflict of laws rule of that country. The court considered the contention that such reference to the whole law would give rise to the endless circle of "renvoi" when the whole law of the forum required reference to the whole law of the situs which referred the matter back to the whole law of the forum, ad infinitum, with no resolution. The court rejected this contention by stating that the problem would not arise where the particular foreign conflicts rule is one which refers to the internal or local law alone and not the whole law. The court decided that a long line of precedent required that the forum court must look to the whole law of the situs, including its conflict of laws rule. It also determined that New York precedents had established that New York recognized the limited concept of "renvoi." The limited version of the concept was stated to be that reference to the law of the domicile meant reference to the local law only. Upon hearing testimony from expert witnesses on the effect of application of the whole law of Switzerland, the court determined that the whole Swiss law would, through its conflict of laws rule, refer the matter to the law of the domicile. Since the local law of the domicile finds no fault with the testamentary disposition established by the deceased, his will shall be recognized as valid and effect given thereto.

▶ ANALYSIS

The concept of "renvoi" as adopted by this court has not been generally followed or approved of. Rather, the position taken by most authorities is that, faced with a conflicts of law problem such as the one in the *Schneider* case, the best resolution is to resort to the local law of the situs and decide the case in that framework. The major criticism of any form of the "renvoi" doctrine is that it creates an untenable legal fiction that creates a lack of uniformity of result. There can be little question that if the property had not been sold and the case adjudicated in the Swiss courts, that they would either have ignored the law of the domicile or applied the "renvoi" doctrine to effect the Swiss law anyway. A somewhat unique problem arises when a foreign court feels compelled to refer to the national or whole law of an American citizen. Should the reference be to the federal law or to the state law of the citizen's domicile? No satisfactory resolution of that problem has ever been arrived at. Similarly, where a conflict arises involving one or more states and the federal government, what law can be applied? In a case involving negligent

Continued on next page.

maintenance of an airplane attributable to the federal government, the plane had been improperly serviced and took off from Oklahoma, but crashed in Missouri. A wrongful death action was brought under the Federal Tort Claims Act. A portion of that Act provided that liability should be determined by the law of the place where the act or omission occurred. Oklahoma did not limit the amount of recovery from wrongful death while Missouri imposed a maximum recovery limitation. An Oklahoma doctrine provided that the whole law of Oklahoma referred the determination of liability and recovery to the place of the injury. Therefore, the Missouri limitation was applied.

■≡■

Quicknotes

SITUS Location; in community property, the location of an asset.

TESTAMENTARY DISPOSITION A disposition of property that is effective upon the death of the grantor.

■≡■

Loucks v. Standard Oil Co. of New York

Estate administrator (P) v. Company (D)

N.Y. Ct. App., 224 N.Y. 99, 120 N.E. 198 (1918).

NATURE OF CASE: Wrongful death suit.

FACT SUMMARY: Loucks was run down and killed in Massachusetts by an employee of Standard Oil (D). His administrator (P) brought a wrongful death suit in New York based on the Massachusetts wrongful death statute.

🏛 RULE OF LAW
A right of action created by a sister state's law is enforceable in any other state unless the law is penal in the international sense or enforcement of the right would violate the strong public policy of the forum.

FACTS: Loucks was killed when he was run down by the negligent driving of an employee of Standard Oil (D). The accident occurred in Massachusetts, but he was a resident of New York, and his administrator (P) brought a suit for wrongful death in that state. The suit was based on the Massachusetts wrongful death statute which provided a minimum recovery of $500 and a maximum recovery of $10,000 with the amount of damages awarded to be based on the degree of culpability of the defendant. Standard Oil (D) moved to dismiss the complaint on the grounds that the Massachusetts Statute was penal in nature and therefore unenforceable in New York.

ISSUE: May a right created in one state by statute be enforced in another state if the enforcement would not violate the public policy of the forum and the underlying statute is not penal in nature?

HOLDING AND DECISION: (Cardozo, J.) Yes. The penal laws of one state are unenforceable in any other. Whether a statute is penal depends on the type of liability it creates. Where the penalty is awarded to the state or a member of the public is suing in the interest of the whole community to redress a public wrong, the statute and/or recovery is penal. While this statute is penal in the sense that damages are awarded on the basis of the defendant's conduct rather than the plaintiff's measure of damages, the right to recover is private and therefore the statute is not penal in the international sense. Enforcement of the right would not violate the public policy of New York, since this state recognizes the right of survivors to recover for wrongful death. The fact that our Statute differs in its mode of enforcement does not make the Massachusetts Statute wrong. The forum may refuse to enforce a right based on a foreign statute only where enforcement would violate an express strong public policy of the forum. That is not the case here and since the Statute is not penal in the international sense, there is no bar to its being enforced in this state. Judgment reversed and order of the Special Term affirmed.

▶ ANALYSIS

Note that the forum has much wider latitude in applying its own public policy to deny relief where the original action is being brought and where it is not a suit on a judgment obtained elsewhere.

■══■

Quicknotes

WRONGFUL DEATH An action brought by the beneficiaries of a deceased person, claiming that the deceased's death was the result of wrongful conduct by the defendant.

■══■

Mertz v. Mertz

Injured passenger (P) v. Husband driver (D)

N.Y. Ct. App., 271 N.Y. 466, 3 N.E.2d 597 (1936).

NATURE OF CASE: Suit for personal injuries.

FACT SUMMARY: Mrs. Mertz (P) brought suit in New York for injuries alleged to have been caused by Mr. Mertz's (D) negligence in a car accident in Connecticut. Connecticut law permitted suits between spouses.

RULE OF LAW
The public policy necessary to deny enforcement of a sister state's statute must be found in the forum's constitution, statutes, or judicial records and not merely in the forum court's own notion of expediency and justice.

FACTS: Mrs. Mertz (P) was injured in Connecticut while riding as a passenger in a car driven by her husband. She brought suit against Mr. Mertz (D) alleging his negligence in New York, the state of their residence. New York had a statute which prohibited a suit by one spouse against the other to recover damages for personal injury. Connecticut had no such statute or policy.

ISSUE: May "public policy" be used as a basis for denying enforcement of a sister state's statute, where such "public policy" is not enunciated in the forum's constitution, statutes, or judicial records?

HOLDING AND DECISION: (Lehman, J.) No. "Public policy" may not be used as a basis for denying enforcement of a sister state's statute, where such "public policy" is not enunciated in the forum's constitution, statutes, or judicial records. While the term "public policy" is ill defined when used in the context of denying enforcement of a sister state's statute, it is capable of some meaningful definition. Properly used "public policy" must be represented by the forum's constitution, statutes, or judicial records. It cannot mean merely the forum court's own notion of expediency or justice. While Connecticut has abandoned the common law concept of one spouse's incapacity to sue the other for personal injury, New York has not. The law of the forum will determine the jurisdiction of the courts, the capacity of the parties to sue or be sued, and the remedies and procedures to be invoked. New York's public policy is to incapacitate one spouse from suing the other without regard for the underlying merit of the cause of action. Connecticut cannot impose its own policy to the contrary on New York. Affirmed.

DISSENT: (Crouch, J.) It is insufficient to say that the public policy of a state can be found in its statutes and judicial records. When the forum is confronted with a sister state statute which is at variance with its own, before "public policy" can be invoked to deny enforcement of the other state's statute, the basic underlying rationale for the existence of the statute must be examined. Where the underlying rationale does not represent good reason, the forum's "public policy" is not sufficiently strong to override a valid sister state statute.

ANALYSIS

The majority opinion would seem to be somewhat at variance with the view expressed by Judge Cardozo in the *Loucks* case, 120 N.E. 198 (1918). Cardozo found that dissimilar statutes pointed toward the same objective were not a conflict of policy. The majority opinion in this case, under its own definition, would find a conflict of policy merely where the statutes conflicted.

Quicknotes

FORUM A court or other location in which a legal remedy may be sought.

PUBLIC POLICY Policy administered by the state with respect to the health, safety and morals of its people in accordance with common notions of fairness and decency.

Holzer v. Deutsche Reichsbahn-Gesellschaft et al.

Employee v. Employer

N.Y. Ct. App., 277 N.Y. 474, 14 N.E.2d 798 (1938).

NATURE OF CASE: Appeal of order striking portions of an answer in action for damages for breach of contract.

FACT SUMMARY: Schenker & Co. (D) raised as a defense to a breach of contract action a law passed by the German government prohibiting the employment of Jews.

🏛 RULE OF LAW
In an action based on breach of an employment contract it may be raised as a defense by the employer that such breach was mandated by law.

FACTS: Holzer (P), a Jewish German, contracted with Schenker & Co. (D), a German corporation, for a term of employment. Prior to expiration of the contract, the German government adopted a law prohibiting the employment of Jews in certain occupations, including that held by Holzer (P). Schenker (D) released Holzer (P), who sued for breach of contract. The trial court, on motion, struck Schenker's (D) defense based on the law promulgated by the German government. Schenker (D) appealed.

ISSUE: In an action based on breach of an employment contract, may it be raised as a defense by the employer that such breach was mandated by law?

HOLDING AND DECISION: (Per curiam) Yes. In an action based on breach of an employment contract, it may be raised as a defense by the employer that such breach was mandated by law. The law of the country where a contract was made must be respected by courts of a forum state. When the law of the state of contract provides a defense to a breach of contract action, that law must be followed by the forum state. Here, the law of Germany not only permitted breach, but mandated it. Therefore, as a matter of law, the contract could not have been breached. Reversed. [The court remanded for a determination of whether the terms of the contract called for payment to Holzer (P) even if he did not perform his contracted-for services.]

▌ ANALYSIS

Courts today are less accepting of foreign law they find repugnant. When foreign law is contrary to public policy, courts are likely not to enforce them. A court today would almost certainly not apply any law like the one of issue here, although it might excuse a contractual performance under a force majeure theory, even though the effect of excuse would be similar to recognition of the repugnant foreign law. It is thus more likely that damages would be awarded.

Quicknotes

FORCE MAJEURE CLAUSE Clause pursuant to an oil and gas lease, relieving the lessee from liability for breach of the lease if the party's performance is impeded as the result of a natural cause that could not have been prevented.

PUBLIC POLICY Policy administered by the state with respect to the health, safety and morals of its people in accordance with common notions of fairness and decency.

■━■

Walton v. Arabian American Oil Co.

Injured motorist (P) v. Car owner (D)

233 F.2d 541 (2d Cir. 1956).

NATURE OF CASE: Personal injury suit.

FACT SUMMARY: Walton (P), an Arkansas resident, was injured when he was struck by a truck owned and operated by Arabian American Oil (D), a Delaware corporation, in Saudi Arabia.

🏛 RULE OF LAW
Courts are not required to take judicial notice of foreign law when it is neither pled nor proved, but may not apply its own law to a foreign tort on the unsupported basis that the country where the accident occurred is "uncivilized."

FACTS: While traveling by car in Saudi Arabia, Walton (P), an Arkansas resident, was struck by a truck owned and operated by Arabian American Oil (D), a Delaware corporation. Walton (P) brought suit in federal district court in New York. At trial, Walton (P) never pled nor offered to prove Arabian "law" on torts. Neither did Arabian American (D). The trial judge refused to take judicial notice of Arabian "law" on his own motion and refused dismissal of the suit.

ISSUE: May a court decide a tort suit, based on an injury incurred in a foreign country, based on the law of the forum, where neither party pleads or proves the applicable foreign law?

HOLDING AND DECISION: (Frank, J.) No. A court may not decide a tort suit, based on an injury incurred in a foreign country, based on the law of the forum, where neither party pleads nor proves the applicable foreign law. As this case is in federal court on diversity jurisdiction, the New York conflict of laws rule is applicable and it holds that the law of the place of the tort is controlling. While New York procedures allow a judge to take judicial notice of foreign law even though neither party proves it, the judge would be abusing his discretion if he were to take notice of a foreign system of laws unfamiliar to our own. Walton (P) asserts that the facts of the incident establish liability under the most "rudimentary" principle of tort law. But there can be no "rudimentary" elements of negligence in the sense they are universally recognized and without proof of Saudi law no decision should have been rendered. New York law requires the plaintiff to go forward to establish the foreign law and this he deliberately failed to do. Finally, Walton argues that Saudi Arabia has no system of laws but claims such as these are decided at the whim of a dictatorial monarch. The assertion that a foreign country is uncivilized or has no system of laws that a civilized country would recognize as adequate must be supported by substantial proof before it will be accepted. The majority of the court feels that since Walton

(P) deliberately refused to prove Saudi law, his complaint should be dismissed. Affirmed.

▶ ANALYSIS

Historically, the presumption was that courts did not know foreign law and if a party desired to rely on foreign law, he must prove it as an issue of fact to the jury. The modern trend is to view the recognition of foreign law as an issue for the judge.

Quicknotes

JUDICIAL NOTICE The discretion of a court to recognize certain well-known facts as being true, without the necessity of a party introducing evidence to establish the truth of the fact.

LEX LOCI The law of the place governs the substantive rights of parties to an action.

Choice of Law: Modern Approaches

Quick Reference Rules of Law

CHAPTER 2

Pritchard v. Norton

Obligee (P) v. Obligor (D)

106 U.S. 124 (1882).

NATURE OF CASE: Suit in contract to enforce payment on indemnity bond.

FACT SUMMARY: Pritchard (P) had gratuitously become a surety on an appeal bond relating to a Louisiana judgment rendered against a railroad. Pritchard (P) had contracted with Norton (D) in New York for Norton (D) to indemnify Pritchard (P) for any loss on the surety.

🏛 RULE OF LAW
Where the parties do not specify which law will be controlling in the event of a dispute in a multistate contract, the terms of the contract and the obligations it imposes will be examined to infer the parties' intent.

FACTS: Pritchard (P) had obligated himself in Louisiana to be a surety on an appeal bond which had to be posted by a railroad in its appeal of an adverse Louisiana judgment. Norton (D) and Pritchard (P) contracted in New York for Norton (D) to indemnify Pritchard (P) against any loss in connection with his suretyship. The railroad lost the appeal and Pritchard (P) was called upon to satisfy the bond. Norton (D) refused to indemnify on the grounds that New York law did not recognize the validity of the indemnity contract. Pritchard (P) asserted that since performance was to be in Louisiana, which recognized the contract, Louisiana law should apply. The trial court rendered a verdict in favor of Norton (D) based on his contention.

ISSUE: Where the parties to a multistate contract do not specify controlling law in the event of a dispute, may the court infer an intent based on the circumstances of the contract?

HOLDING AND DECISION: (Matthews, J.) Yes. Where the parties to a multistate contract do not specify controlling law in the event of a dispute, the court may infer an intent based on the circumstances of the contract. It must be presumed that parties to a contract will not enter into an agreement that is not enforceable. Since the surety of Pritchard (P) arose in Louisiana and any indemnity payment must be made there, the law of Louisiana must have been intended by the parties to be applicable. Where an obligor assumes an obligation, he must intend that the law which would uphold the obligation will be controlling in the event of a dispute over performance. The place of the contracting will not be material where it is different than the place of performance. Reversed with directions to grant a new trial.

▶ ANALYSIS

The decision seems to rest on the doctrine of validating a contract wherever possible. Since persons who enter into a contract do so with the expectation it will be fulfilled, they do not, in reality, intend any law to govern disputes. The Court's decision and rationale would allow the courts to pick whichever law the courts thought should apply resorting to the legal fiction of inferring the parties' intent.

■■■

Quicknotes

BOND A written instrument evidencing a debt that is issued by a party to the bondholder, providing for interest payments to be made over a specific time period and promising to repay the debt upon specified terms.

CONSIDERATION Value given by one party in exchange for performance, or a promise to perform, by another party.

INDEMNITY The duty of a party to compensate another for damages sustained.

SURETY A party who guarantees payment of the debt of another party to a creditor.

■■■

Siegelman v. Cunard White Star Ltd.

Injured passenger v. Ship

221 F.2d 189 (2d Cir. 1955).

NATURE OF CASE: Suit for personal injuries received aboard an ocean liner.

FACT SUMMARY: Mrs. Siegelman (P) was injured while crossing the Atlantic Ocean aboard a Cunard (D) ship. The ticket of passage contained a clause requiring suits for injury to be brought within one year and that all disputes arising out of the contract would be decided by reference to English law.

🏛 RULE OF LAW
The parties to a contract may stipulate therein which law will govern disputes as to interpretation or validity of the contract so long as the choice is bona fide and relates to either the execution or performance of the contract.

FACTS: Mrs. Siegelman (P) and her husband purchased an Atlantic crossing ticket from Cunard Lines (D) in New York. The ticket, which was in the form of a contract, contained three clauses relevant to this case. One was that any action for death or injury to a passenger must be filed within one year from the date of the accident. The second stated that all questions arising on the contract would be decided in accordance with English law. The third clause stated that any alterations of the contract terms of Cunard (D) liability must be in writing. Mrs. Siegelman (P) was injured while on the high seas and a claim for reimbursement was filed. The one-year deadline approached before settlement of the claim and a Cunard (D) claims agent stated, when asked, that suit would not have to be filed since there was an excellent chance of settlement. Mrs. Siegelman (P) subsequently died and Cunard (D) then denied any recovery on the basis that Mrs. Siegelman's (P) claim did not survive her. Mr. Siegelman (P) then filed suit past the one-year time limit, asserting waiver of the limit by the claims agent. Citing the contract terms, the district court dismissed the suit on motion by Cunard (D).

ISSUE: Where the parties to a multistate or international contract have stipulated as to which law will govern validity, interpretation or both, will that stipulation, assuming it is reasonable, be given effect by the court?

HOLDING AND DECISION: (Harlan, J.) Yes. Where the parties to a multistate or international contract have stipulated as to which law will govern validity, interpretation, or both, that stipulation, assuming it is reasonable, will be given effect by the court. The case will be decided in the context of federal rather than state law, since it involves maritime jurisdiction. This case presents issues on contract, not tort. The intent of the parties, as evidenced by the contract, is that English law should control. This intent will be given force where applicable. The parties may always stipulate

as to which law will govern interpretation, since this will involve no more than a stipulation of definitions. The stipulation as to validity, however, is an attempt to usurp the proper legislative authority of a state to determine validity. It will be recognized only insofar as it does not conflict with that valid authority. The choice of law so stipulated must bear a reasonable relationship to either the place of the making or of performance of the contract. Therefore, the selection of the applicable law as to validity will not automatically be validated but can be recognized by the court in its discretion. The question of the claims agent's purported waiver is more closely related to validity rather than interpretation. As such, it should be considered under applicable English law which we read as holding such verbal waiver ineffective. The trial court's dismissal of the suit was, therefore, proper. Affirmed.

DISSENT: (Frank, J.) The contract clause referred to suits brought on the contract. This suit arises out of post contract behavior and should not be governed by the terms of the contract. Even if it were governable by the contract, the reference to English law is sufficiently ambiguous as to its application that it should be disregarded. Further, this is a contract of adhesion since it was offered on a take it or leave it basis by a party in a superior bargaining position. This issue of waiver should have been determined in accordance with internal American law.

▶ ANALYSIS

Choice of law stipulations in contracts will usually be given effect unless it is clearly unreasonable to do so. The rationale usually advanced is intent of the parties and minimization of litigation. The Uniform Commercial Code specifically sanctions choice of laws provisions in contracts so long as the law chosen bears a reasonable relationship to the parties and/or the contract. With the wide adoption of the U.C.C. in this country, the number of cases relating to effectiveness of such contract clauses has dropped off sharply. The Second Restatement also adopts the position validating reasonable choice of law preselections. The proviso is always present, however, that the choice must relate in some reasonable manner to the parties or the contract. The adhesion contract theory expressed in the dissent above has been used to invalidate choice of law clauses where the weaker party to a contract is greatly disadvantaged by the clause.

■=■

Quicknotes

ADHESION CONTRACT A contract, usually in standardized form, that is prepared by one party and offered to another,

Continued on next page.

whose terms are so disproportionately in favor of the drafting party that courts tend to question the equality of bargaining power in reaching the agreement.

ESTOPPEL An equitable doctrine precluding a party from asserting a right to the detriment of another who justifiably relied on the conduct.

WAIVER The intentional or voluntary forfeiture of a recognized right.

■≡■

Wyatt v. Fulrath

Husband's executor v. Wife's executor

N.Y. Ct. App., 16 N.Y.2d 169, 211 N.E.2d 637 (1965).

NATURE OF CASE: Action for an accounting and claim of title.

FACT SUMMARY: Spanish nationals sent personal property to New York whose law allows for all property to go to a survivor spouse while Spanish law allows only half to go to the survivor.

RULE OF LAW
A marital property contract may determine the law to be applied to the property acquired during the marriage if the contract is validly made and if the property is within the jurisdiction of the law to be applied.

FACTS: A husband and wife were nationals and domiciliaries of Spain. As a result of the political instability leading up to the Spanish Civil War, they sent cash and securities to New York. Neither of them ever went to New York. In 1957, the husband died. The wife later transferred some property held in a joint account in London to New York. In 1959, the wife died. The husband and wife had agreed that the New York law of survivorship would apply to these funds under which the total amount of property went to the survivor. Spanish law provided that only half of the property would go to the survivor. Wyatt (P), the husband's executor, sued Fulrath (D), the wife's executor, for half of the funds over which the wife took total control upon the husband's death.

ISSUE: May a marital property contract determine the law to be applied to the property acquired during the marriage if the contract is validly made and if the property is within the jurisdiction of the law to be applied?

HOLDING AND DECISION: (Bergan, J.) Yes. A state has the right to say as a matter of public policy whether it will apply its own law to foreigners who choose to place property there for custody and protection. The property was sent to New York and the parties manifested the intent that New York law and not Spanish law should be applied to the disposition of the property. This factor of intent outweighs the facts that the parties had never been in New York, had not executed their agreement in New York, and were nationals of Spain. However, the money that was sent to London and then to New York by the wife comes under a different rule. The law of England must determine whether this money passed to the wife on the husband's death, or whether England would apply Spanish law to these facts. Affirmed as modified.

DISSENT: (Desmond, C.J.) The law of the matrimonial domicile has traditionally controlled devolution and property rights. The parties had no contact with New York other than sending their money there for bailment. The forms that the bank had the parties sign for joint accounts were meant merely to protect the bank and they do not indicate an intent to abrogate the law of Spain.

ANALYSIS
Where the contract indicates a manifested intent for another law to be applied, and if the property is in that other jurisdiction, public policy considerations may lead to the enforcement of that jurisdiction's laws.

Quicknotes

BAILMENT The delivery of property to be held in trust and which is designated for a particular purpose, following the satisfaction of which the property is either to be returned or disposed of as specified.

COMMUNITY PROPERTY In community property jurisdictions, refers to all money or property acquired during the term of the marriage in which each spouse has an undivided one-half interest.

JOINT BANK ACCOUNT A bank account in which two or more persons have equal interests usually with right of survivorship.

PUBLIC POLICY Policy administered by the state with respect to the health, safety and morals of its people in accordance with common notions of fairness and decency.

Chesny v. Marek

Civil rights litigant (P) v. Offeror (D)

720 F.2d 474 (7th Cir. 1983).

NATURE OF CASE: Appeal from order setting costs pursuant to judgment in federal civil rights action.

FACT SUMMARY: In a federal civil rights action, Marek (D) contended that a Fed. R. Civ. P. 68 offer precluded the awarding of attorney fees to Chesny (P), who received a judgment for less than the amount of the offer.

🏛 RULE OF LAW
A Fed. R. Civ. P. 68 offer may not preclude the awarding of attorney fees under 42 U.S.C. § 1988.

FACTS: Chesny (P) brought a federal civil rights action against various defendants, alleging excessive use of force. At one point near trial, a Fed. R. Civ. P. 68 offer of $100,000 to settle was made. Chesny (P) rejected it, and the case went to trial. The jury awarded $60,000. The district court, pursuant to 42 U.S.C. § 1988, awarded Chesny (P) attorney fees, but not for the time after the Rule 68 offer was rejected, ruling that Chesny's (P) lesser verdict precluded such an award. Chesny (P) appealed.

ISSUE: May a Fed. R. Civ. P. 68 offer preclude the awarding of attorney fees under 42 U.S.C. § 1988?

HOLDING AND DECISION: (Posner, J.) No. A Fed. R. Civ. P. 68 offer may not preclude the awarding of attorney fees under 42 U.S.C. § 1988. Fed. R. Civ. P. 68 provides that when a defendant makes an offer to allow judgment to be entered, and a plaintiff rejects same, the offeree must pay the defendant's costs for the period following rejection. Section 1988 provides for a successful plaintiff in a civil rights action to recover attorney fees. The question is whether Fed. R. Civ. P. 68 prohibits a successful plaintiff from recovering his fees under § 1988. This court believes it does not. Rule 68 only speaks of "costs"; attorney fees are distinct from costs. Beyond that, 42 U.S.C. § 1988 was enacted to encourage meritorious civil rights actions; to allow Rule 68 to prohibit the awarding of such costs would undercut the policies behind § 1988. The Rules Enabling Act, 28 U.S.C. § 2072, provides that the Federal Rules of Civil Procedure should not be construed to abridge substantive rights. The construction of Rule 68 as urged by Marek (D) would do this. Affirmed in part, reversed in part, and remanded.

▶ ANALYSIS

Section 1988 was enacted by Congress in 1976 based on the perception that the federal government lacked the resources to investigate all incidents of civil rights violations. Its purpose was to encourage meritorious civil litigation.

■▬■

Marek v. Chesny

Offeror (D) v. Civil rights litigant (P)

473 U.S. 1 (1985).

NATURE OF CASE: Review of order setting costs pursuant to judgment in federal civil rights action.

FACT SUMMARY: In a federal civil rights action, Marek (D) contended that a Fed. R. Civ. P. 68 offer precluded the awarding of attorney fees to Chesny (P), who received a judgment for less than the amount of the offer.

🏛 RULE OF LAW
A Fed. R. Civ. P. 68 offer may preclude the awarding of attorney fees under 42 U.S.C. § 1988.

FACTS: Chesny (P) brought a federal civil rights action against various defendants, alleging excessive use of force. As trial approached, a Fed. R. Civ. P. 68 offer of $100,000 to settle was made, which Chesny (P) rejected. The case went to trial, and a jury awarded $60,000. The district court, pursuant to 42 U.S.C. § 1988, awarded Chesny (P) attorney fees, but not for the period after the Rule 68 offer had been rejected, ruling that Chesny's (P) lesser verdict precluded such an award. The Seventh Circuit reversed, and the Supreme Court granted review.

ISSUE: May a Fed. R. Civ. P. 68 offer preclude the awarding of attorney fees under 42 U.S.C. § 1988?

HOLDING AND DECISION: (Burger, C.J.) Yes. A Fed. R. Civ. P. 68 offer may preclude the awarding of attorney fees under 42 U.S.C. § 1988. Fed. R. Civ. P. 68 provides that when a defendant makes an offer which is rejected, the defendant will not be liable for the plaintiff's costs after the date of rejection. Section 1988 states that attorney fees may be awarded to a prevailing plaintiff as part of his costs. Thus, under a clear reading of the two provisions, Rule 68 would appear to impact on § 1988. It is argued, however, that applying Rule 68 to § 1988 would frustrate the purpose behind the latter section. This Court disagrees. Section 1988 only provides for awarding "reasonable" attorney fees. If a reasonable offer is rejected, it stands to reason that fees incurred thereafter are not reasonable. In essence, § 1988 exists to encourage meritorious suits, and Rule 68 exists to encourage settlement. These sections do not conflict with each other. Reversed.

▶ ANALYSIS

When one thinks of conflicts of laws, the scenario that usually comes to mind is that of competing laws of different jurisdictions. However, when different laws of the same jurisdiction would tend to work against each other, in a sense a conflict exists. The usual method for resolving such conflicts is to look first to the language of the competing laws and, secondly, to attempt to divine legislative intent.

Quicknotes

COST An amount that is considered the equivalent in value for an item of goods or an activity or event.

42 U.S.C. § 1988 Allows for attorney fees to be awarded the prevailing party in an action pursuant to § 1983.

Tooker v. Lopez

Estate administrator (P) v. Automobile driver (D)

N.Y. Ct. App., 24 N.Y.2d 569, 249 N.E.2d 394 (1969).

NATURE OF CASE: Appeal from dismissal of personal injury and wrongful death action.

FACT SUMMARY: The Michigan trial court dismissed a civil action arising out of an accident that occurred in Michigan but involved a New York vehicle and only New York domiciliaries.

🏛 RULE OF LAW
When an accident occurs in one state but all the persons involved are citizens of another, the law of that other state applies.

FACTS: Lopez and Tooker were involved in an auto accident in which Lopez, the driver, lost control of her vehicle. Both were killed. They had both been New York domiciliaries residing in Michigan while attending Michigan State University. The vehicle was registered and insured in New York. Tooker's estate (P) and her parents (P) brought a personal injury/wrongful death action against Lopez's estate (D). The trial court, applying Michigan's guest statute, dismissed, holding that Michigan had no interest in the matter as all the parties were New York domiciliaries. The appellate division affirmed, and the court of appeals granted review.

ISSUE: When an accident occurs in one state but all the persons involved are citizens of another, does the law of that other state apply?

HOLDING AND DECISION: (Keating, J.) Yes. When an accident occurs in one state but all the persons involved are citizens of another, the law of that other state applies. The traditional lex loci delicti rule, which provided that the law of the jurisdiction of accident invariably controls, is no longer followed. Rather, courts of this state now look to which state has the greater interest. When all the litigants involved in a particular accident are citizens of a state other than that where the accident occurred, it is highly unlikely that the locus state will have a valid interest in the application of its law. The present case is an example. The stated purpose of the guest statute is to protect local insurers from fraudulent, collusive claims. This may be a valid policy, but Michigan has no interest in an out-of-state carrier, as is involved here. As Michigan has no interest here, the accident's occurrence there being purely adventitious, Michigan has no interest in its guest statute being applied here. Order of Appellate Division reversed and order of Special Term reinstated.

CONCURRENCE: (Fuld, C.J.) The following principles arise from this case: (1) When the passenger and driver live in the same state, and the car is registered there, the law of that state controls. (2) When the driver's offensive conduct

occurs in the state in which he lives, and that state imposes no liability for that conduct, he cannot be held liable even if the liability would be imposed under law of the state of the victim's domicile. And if the guest is injured in the state of his own domicile, and that state permits recovery, the driver that came into the state should generally not be permitted to use the law of his state for a defense. (3) When the passenger and driver are from different states, the rule will generally be that of the state where the accident occurred unless substituting another rule will advance the relevant substantive law without impairing the working of the multi-state system.

DISSENT: (Breitel, J.) Here, it was the citizenship of the parties and the state of registration that was "purely adventitious."

▶ ANALYSIS

The threshold exercise in which one must engage in conflicts analysis is identification of a conflict. The mere existence of overlapping jurisdictions in a situation does not in itself a conflict make; there must be competing interests involved. Here, the court of appeals believed that Michigan had no interest at all.

Quicknotes

DOMICILE A person's permanent home or principal establishment to which he has an intention of returning when he is absent therefrom.

GUEST STATUTE A state statute requiring a specified level of culpability, usually more than mere negligence, on the part of the driver of an automobile in order to be liable for injuries resulting to a gratuitous passenger.

LEX LOCI DELICTI Refers to the location in which the unlawful activity giving rise to liability occurred.

WRONGFUL DEATH An action brought by the beneficiaries of a deceased person, claiming that the deceased's death was the result of wrongful conduct by the defendant.

Schultz v. Boy Scouts of America, Inc.

Father (P) v. Boys' charity group (D)

N.Y. Ct. App., 65 N.Y.2d 189, 480 N.E.2d 679 (1985).

NATURE OF CASE: Appeal from grant of defense motion for summary judgment based on New Jersey immunity statute in action involving New York tort.

FACT SUMMARY: In an action among New Jersey domiciliaries, the trial court applied New Jersey charitable immunity law to tortious conduct in New York.

RULE OF LAW
The lex loci delicti rule will not apply when all parties are domiciled in the same foreign state.

FACTS: All parties were domiciled in New Jersey. Schultz's (P) sons were allegedly molested in New York by a scoutmaster affiliated with the Boy Scouts (D), leading one son to suicide. New Jersey had a charitable immunity statute; New York did not. The case was summarily adjudicated under New Jersey law. Schultz (P) appealed.

ISSUE: Should the lex loci delicti rule apply when all parties are domiciled in the same foreign state?

HOLDING AND DECISION: (Simons, J.) No. The lex loci delicti rule will not apply when all parties are domiciled in the same foreign state. Lex loci delicti usually predominates if the issue in conflict is conduct-regulating. This case presents a loss-allocating conflict, and analysis favors applying the law of the common domicile. This approach reduces forum-shopping and promotes certainty; it protects the parties' expectations on applicable law. New York public policy is not implicated in this case because no significant contacts exist among the parties, the tort, and this forum. Affirmed.

DISSENT: (Jasen, J.) Boy Scouts (D) has changed domiciles, and there is little interest in shielding them under New Jersey immunity laws. By contrast, New York has a paramount interest in preventing child sexual abuse. This case rests almost exclusively on the Schultzes' (P) domicile, so visiting nonresidents are less protected by our laws. But the parties were not in transit through New York; their stay availed them to New York protections and obligations. Indeed, it would cause surprise to know that one's conduct while in New York was not governed by state laws. Lex loci should not be indiscriminately disregarded.

ANALYSIS

Contrary to the dissent's position, a post-tort change of residence is irrelevant for conflicts analysis. The parties' domiciles at the time of injury generally control. This case shows that courts rarely refuse to apply foreign law based on public policy grounds. "The courts are not free to refuse to enforce a foreign right at the pleasure of the judges." *Loucks v. Standard Oil*, 224 N.Y. 99, 120 N.E. 198 (1918).

Quicknotes

DOMICILE A person's permanent home or principal establishment to which he has an intention of returning when he is absent therefrom.

FORUM-SHOPPING Refers to a situation in which one party to an action seeks to have the matter heard and determined by a court, or in a jurisdiction, that will provide it with the most favorable result.

IMMUNITY Exemption from a legal obligation.

LEX LOCI DELICTI Refers to the location in which the unlawful activity giving rise to liability occurred.

SUMMARY JUDGMENT Judgment rendered by a court in response to a motion by one of the parties, claiming that the lack of a question of material fact in respect to an issue warrants disposition of the issue without consideration by the jury.

Erwin v. Thomas

Injured Washington resident (P) v. Oregon resident (D)

Or. Sup. Ct., 264 Or. 454, 506 P.2d 494 (1973).

NATURE OF CASE: Appeal from dismissal of an action by a wife for loss of consortium.

FACT SUMMARY: Erwin's (P) husband, a Washington resident, was injured in Washington by Thomas (D), an Oregon resident, for which Erwin (P) sued in Oregon for loss of her husband's consortium, a cause of action unavailable to wives in Washington.

🏛 RULE OF LAW

When no state has a legitimate interest in the application of its law in the trial of an action, the law of the forum state should be applied.

FACTS: Erwin (P) and her husband were Washington residents. Thomas (D), an Oregon resident, was in the course and scope of his employment for an Oregon corporation, Shepler (D), when he, by his negligent operation of a Shepler (D) truck, caused Erwin's (P) husband's injury. Erwin (P) brought suit in Oregon for loss of her husband's consortium. Thomas (D) moved to dismiss on grounds that Washington law should apply, and that Washington provides no cause of action to a wife for loss of her husband's consortium. Oregon does provide such a cause of action to wives. This trial court dismissed the action, and Erwin (P) appealed.

ISSUE: When no state has a legitimate interest in the application of its law in the trial of an action, should the law of the forum state be applied?

HOLDING AND DECISION: (Holman, J.) Yes. When no state has a legitimate interest in the application of its law in the trial of an action, the law of the forum state should be applied. The interests of the two states in question, Washington and Oregon, must first be determined. Washington does not believe the rights of a married woman to be sufficiently important to provide her a remedy. But Washington policy cannot be offended if another state's court gives rights to a Washington resident which Washington does not give so long as no Washington defendant is involved. Thus, Washington would appear to have no urgent policy or interest which would be offended by application of Oregon Law. Oregon, on the other hand, protects a married woman's interest. However, it does not seem that Oregon had in mind the protection of all nonresident, married women injured outside the state of Oregon. There being no legitimate interest held by either state, the law of the forum, Oregon, should apply. Where policies and interests can be determined with a fair degree of certainty and there appears no true conflict, it is unnecessary to use the "most significant relationship" test of the Second Restatement of Conflicts. Reversed and remanded.

DISSENT: (Bryson, J.) Oregon statutory rights should not be given nonresidents who simply walk across the border. The policies of Washington and Oregon obviously conflict if the former will not provide a remedy while the latter will.

▶ ANALYSIS

The decision above raises the question of the "unprovided-for case." What law should apply when two states have conflicting law, but there is no overriding interest which points to one or the other as legitimate? Some suggest that the law of the forum should apply. That is the view of Professor Currie, the prime proponent of interest analysis, which he bases on the reason that there is then no purpose in displacing the forum's law with any other. Professor Sedler suggests that some common policy can be discerned between the forums which would indicate the law to be applied.

■═■

Quicknotes

LEX LOCI DELICTI The law governing the location in which an unlawful activity, giving rise to a cause of action, took place.

RENVOI A doctrine pursuant to which a court adopts the conflict of law rules of a foreign jurisdiction, which requires the court to apply to the laws of its own forum.

■═■

Lilienthal v. Kaufman

Lender (P) v. Borrower (D)

Or. Sup. Ct., 239 Or. 1, 395 P.2d 543 (1964).

NATURE OF CASE: Action to enforce payment of promissory notes.

FACT SUMMARY: Kaufman (D), an Oregon resident, had been declared a spendthrift under Oregon law and a guardian was appointed for his protection. He went to California, where he borrowed money from Lilienthal (P) to finance a business venture.

🏛 RULE OF LAW
Where two states have an equal balance of interests in application of their own laws to an interstate contract dispute, the forum is privileged to apply its own law so as to advance its own public policy.

FACTS: Under a statutory procedure in Oregon, Kaufman (D) had been declared a spendthrift and a guardian appointed to manage his affairs to prevent waste of his assets to the detriment of himself and his family. By the terms of the statute, any contracts made by the spendthrift after the appointment of the guardian were voidable by the guardian. Kaufman (D) traveled from his home in Oregon to San Francisco where he induced Lilienthal (P) to advance him money for a business venture. Lilienthal (P) was unaware of Kaufman's (D) disability and when he sought to enforce repayment of the promissory notes in an Oregon court, the guardian declared the obligations void and unenforceable. California law did not recognize a spendthrift's disability to contract.

ISSUE: May the forum apply its own law to advance its own public policy where there is an equal balance of conflicting interests in the choice of law in an interstate contract dispute?

HOLDING AND DECISION: (Denecke, J.) Yes. The forum may apply its own law to advance its own public policy where there is an equal balance of conflicting interests in the choice of law in a contract dispute. In a previous case involving Kaufman (D) as a defendant in a similar suit brought by an Oregon resident, this court held that the guardianship acted as a bar to enforcement of the obligations. The court is now faced, however, with the conflicting interests of California in protecting its own creditors. Further, there is the traditional rule that the law of the place where a contract is made will govern its validity. There is authority for the assertion that choice of law should be made in a manner that upholds, not voids, a contract. Oregon has an interest in seeing that contracts made by its citizens are honored in Oregon courts. Balanced against these considerations is the valid public policy, expressed by the legislation, of preventing a spendthrift from making himself and his family public charges by his wastrel ways. The Oregon legislation must be presumed to have considered the adverse consequences of the spendthrift disability on interstate commerce when choosing to grant this form of immunity. When faced with such an equal balance of interests, the courts of this state are under an obligation to give force to the express public policy. Toward that end we find the obligations unenforceable. Affirmed.

CONCURRENCE: (O'Connell, J.) In view of our previous decision barring recovery by an Oregon creditor, I see no need to afford greater protection to an out-of-state creditor.

DISSENT: (Goodwin, J.) The overriding policy of both Oregon and California to uphold the sanctity of contracts has been lost in the decision to keep the rare spendthrift off the welfare rolls of Oregon. It is a step back toward Balkanization to send an out-of-state creditor toward insolvency to uphold a dubious policy of Oregon.

▶ ANALYSIS

The case represents an example of Currie's approach to choice of law that emphasizes the importance of the forum's law. The Oregon court was quick to find that there was a balance of conflicting interests, and in the face of that balance that the forum should prevail. There has been criticism of this case on the ground that, while an Oregon creditor is presumed to know Oregon law, a California creditor must be presumed to act on his knowledge of California law. The Oregon statute is not so commonplace as to be regarded as within the reasonable contemplation of the out-of-state creditor.

Quicknotes

CALIFORNIA CODE OF CIV. PROC., § 1913 Authority of a guardian does not extend beyond jurisdiction.

LEX LOCI CONTRACTUS The place in which a contract was entered or the place where the contract is to be performed, designating the law pursuant to which the contract is to be governed.

SPENDTHRIFT A person who spends money excessively and unwisely.

Bernkrant v. Fowler

Property buyer (P) v. Vendor's estate (D)

Cal. Sup. Ct., 55 Cal. 2d 588, 360 P.2d 906 (1961).

NATURE OF CASE: Appeal from denial of enforcement of an oral contract.

FACT SUMMARY: Granrud, a vendor of land in Nevada, made an oral agreement with Bernkrant (P) and other purchasers that if they paid a substantial part of their indebtedness before the due date he would provide by will for the cancellation of any remaining indebtedness, but Granrud died without providing for such cancellation in the will.

RULE OF LAW
The basic policy of enforcing lawful contracts made under the law of the state of execution precludes the application of the forum's Statute of Frauds when the application arises from the movement of contracting parties across state lines.

FACTS: A vendor of Nevada land, Granrud, asked Bernkrant (P) and the other purchasers to refinance their obligations and to pay a substantial part of their indebtedness before the due date. He promised orally that if Bernkrant (P) and the others did this he would provide by will that any part of the purchase price remaining unpaid on his death would be canceled. Bernkrant (P) and the others complied with the request. The vendor died with about $6,000 of the purchase money unpaid, but his will made no provision for cancellation of the debt. The purchasers brought an action in California against Fowler (D), the vendor's executor, to enforce the oral agreement. Under Nevada law where the agreement was transacted, such an oral contract was valid. Under California law, such a transaction is invalid unless written. The trial court gave judgment for Fowler (D) and Bernkrant (P) appealed.

ISSUE: Does the basic policy of enforcing lawful contracts made under the law of the state of execution preclude the application of the forum's Statute of Frauds when the application arises from the movement of contracting parties across state lines?

HOLDING AND DECISION: (Traynor, J.) Yes. The basic policy of enforcing lawful contracts made under the law of the state of execution precludes the application of the forum's Statute of Frauds when the application arises from the movement of contracting parties across state lines. The contract is valid under the laws of Nevada where it was executed and performed but invalid under the California Statute of Frauds if that Statute is applicable. There is no doubt that California's interest in protecting estates being probated here from false claims based on alleged oral contracts to make wills is constitutionally sufficient to justify making our Statute of Frauds applicable to all such contracts. The legislature, however, is ordinarily concerned with enacting laws to govern purely local transactions, and it has not spelled out the extent to which the Statute of Frauds is to apply to a contract having substantial contacts with another state. In the present case, Bernkrant (P) and the others were residents of Nevada; the contract was made in Nevada, and performed there. If Granrud was a resident of Nevada at the time the contract was made, the California Statute of Frauds would not apply even though Granrud subsequently moved to California. The basic policy of upholding the expectations of the parties by enforcing contracts valid under the law of the state where the transaction took place would preclude an interpretation of the Statute of Frauds that would make it apply to and thus invalidate the contract because of the movement of one or more of the parties across state lines. In the present case, however, there is no finding as to where Granrud was domiciled at the time the contract was made and thus the plaintiffs could not be expected to have been alerted to the Statute of Frauds. Reversed.

ANALYSIS

Apparently, even if Granrud was domiciled in California, the result would be the same because the contract was made in Nevada and performed by plaintiffs there, and it involved the refinancing of obligations arising from the sale of Nevada land and secured by interests therein. Therefore, concludes the court, Nevada has a substantial interest in the contract and in protecting the rights of its residents who are parties thereto.

■■■

Quicknotes

DOMICILE A person's permanent home or principal establishment to which he has an intention of returning when he is absent therefrom.

STATUTE OF FRAUDS A statute that requires specified types of contracts to be in writing in order to be binding.

■■■

Bernhard v. Harrah's Club

Injured cyclist (P) v. Casino (D)

Cal. Sup. Ct., 16 Cal. 3d 313, 546 P.2d 719 (1976).

NATURE OF CASE: Appeal from an action for damages for personal injuries.

FACT SUMMARY: Two Californians patronized Harrah's Club (D), a Nevada corporation, where they became intoxicated and then collided with a motorcycle operated by Bernhard (P), in California.

🏛 RULE OF LAW
A conflict in the choice of law governing a tort action requires an analysis of the respective interests of the states involved, the objective of which is to determine the law that most appropriately applies to the issue involved.

FACTS: Bernhard (P) brought an action in California for damages for personal injuries against Harrah's Club (D), a Nevada corporation. Bernhard (P) alleged that Harrah's Club (D), which owned and operated gambling and drinking establishments in Nevada, solicited business in California, knowing that many Californians would use the highways in going to and from Harrah's Club (D). In response to Harrah's Club (D) advertisements, two Californians patronized the establishment, became obviously intoxicated and, on their way home, a car driven by one of the intoxicated Californians collided with a motorcycle operated by Bernhard (P), also a California resident, who suffered severe injuries. Harrah's Club (D) demurred to Bernhard's (P) complaint on the ground that Nevada law gave no right to recover against a tavern keeper for injuries caused by the selling of alcoholic beverages to an intoxicated person and that Nevada law governed since Bernhard's (P) alleged tort had been committed in Nevada. The trial court sustained the demurrer and Bernhard (P) appealed.

ISSUE: Does a conflict in the choice of law governing a tort action require an analysis of the respective interests of the states involved in order to determine the law that most appropriately applies to the issue involved?

HOLDING AND DECISION: (Sullivan, J.) Yes. As this court has made clear on other occasions, it no longer adheres to the rule that the law of the place of the wrong is applicable in a California forum regardless of the issues before the court. Rather, a rule has been adopted requiring an analysis of the respective interests of the states involved, the objective of which is to determine the law that most appropriately applies to the issue involved. The laws of California and Nevada applicable to the issue involved are not identical. California imposes liability on tavern keepers in this state for conduct as here alleged, Nevada does not. Harrah's Club (D) contends that Nevada has a definite interest in having its

rule of decision applied in this case in order to protect its resident tavern keepers from being subjected to a civil liability which Nevada has not imposed either by legislative enactment or decisional law. Bernhard (P), on the other hand, points out that California has an interest in protecting members of the general public from injuries to person and damage to property resulting from the excessive use of intoxicating liquor. Thus, since this case involved a California resident injured in this state by intoxicated drivers and a Nevada resident tavern keeper, it is clear that each state has an interest in the application of its respective laws. Furthermore, this court finds that the act of selling alcoholic beverages to obviously intoxicated persons is already proscribed in Nevada, which subjects tavern keepers to criminal penalties. Therefore, the application of the California rule of civil liability would not impose an entirely new duty requiring the ability to distinguish between California residents and other patrons. The conclusion is that California has an important interest in applying its law, which would be more significantly impaired if such a rule were not applied. The judgment is reversed and the case remanded.

▶ ANALYSIS

In reaching its decision the court also used the comparative impairment approach to the resolution of conflicts. This approach seeks to determine which state's interest would be more impaired if its policy were subordinated to the policy of the other state. The court does not weigh the conflicting governmental interests in the sense of determining which conflicting law manifested the better or the worthier social policy on the specific issue.

■━■

Quicknotes

DEMURRAL The assertion that the opposing party's pleadings are insufficient and that the demurring party should not be made to answer.

■━■

Phillips v. General Motors Corp.

Decedents' estate (P) v. Manufacturer (D)

Mont. Sup. Ct., 298 Mont. 438, 995 P.2d 1002 (2000).

NATURE OF CASE: Certified questions regarding Montana's choice of law rule.

FACT SUMMARY: Phillips (P), the legal guardian of the sole survivor of a traffic accident and personal representative of the estates of the survivor's parents who perished in the crash, sued General Motors (GM) (D) for personal injury, product liability, and wrongful death in Montana, where the accident victims resided.

🏛 RULE OF LAW
Where there is a potential conflict of laws, Montana will follow the most significant relationship test in determining which state's substantive law to apply.

FACTS: Phillips (P) represented the estates of a Montana family killed while driving a Chevrolet pickup truck on a freeway in Kansas while on the way to spend Christmas in North Carolina. Phillips (P), who lived in North Carolina, filed suit for product liability in federal court in Montana. When the parties disagreed on which state's substantive law applied, the court certified three questions to the Montana Supreme Court.

ISSUE: Where there is a potential conflict of laws, will Montana follow the most significant relationship test in determining which state's substantive law to apply?

HOLDING AND DECISION: (Regnier, J.) Yes. Where there is a potential conflict of laws, Montana will follow the most significant relationship test in determining which state's substantive law to apply. Under the Restatement (Second) of Conflict of Laws approach that the Court now adopts, the local law of the place of injury, Kansas, is presumptively applicable in a product liability and wrongful death action unless another state has a more significant relationship. The following factors all point to the application of Montana law: the deceased resided in Montana at the time of the accident, GM (D) does business in Montana, Montana has a direct interest in preventing defective products from injuring Montana residents and is interested in fully compensating Montana residents. The public policies of all interested states must be considered in determining which state has the more significant relationship; a "public policy" exception would therefore be redundant. Since the lex loci rule has been abandoned for contract disputes, the same choice of law approach should also be applied in tort cases.

▶ ANALYSIS

The court carefully considered each of the factors set out in Restatement (Second). They included: needs of the interstate and international system, the policies of interested states, place of injury, place of conduct, residence of parties, and basic policies underlying the particular field of law. North Carolina would not have applied its own laws because it still adhered to the traditional place of injury rule in tort cases.

■══■

Quicknotes

LEX LOCI The law of the place governs the substantive rights of parties to an action.

PRODUCT LIABILITY The legal liability of manufacturers and sellers for damages and injuries suffered by buyers, users, and even bystanders because of defects in goods purchased.

■══■

Wood Bros. Homes, Inc. v. Walker Adjustment Bureau

Owner (D) v. Builder (P)

Colo. Sup. Ct., 198 Colo. 444, 601 P.2d 1369 (1979).

NATURE OF CASE: Action to recover for breach of contract.

FACT SUMMARY: Walker's (P) assignor, a California resident, had contracted to do some work on a New Mexico apartment complex owned by Wood Bros. (D), a Delaware corporation having its principal place of business in Colorado.

🏛 RULE OF LAW
The Restatement (Second) of Conflict of Laws would resolve any particular issue by applying the law of that state having the "most significant relationship" to that issue and adopts a rebuttable presumption that the state where services are to be performed is the state having the most significant relationship to the issue of the validity of the contract.

FACTS: Pursuant to negotiations in California, Colorado, and New Mexico, Wood Bros. (D) contracted to have Gagnon, a California resident, perform rough carpentry work on an apartment complex it owned in New Mexico. After some of the work was begun, New Mexico officials ordered construction halted because Gagnon had no New Mexico contractor's license. Wood (D) canceled the contract and refused to pay Gagnon, although it did pay his employees some $27,000 for their work. As Gagnon's assignee, Walker (P) brought suit in Colorado for recovery on either a contract or quantum meruit theory. The trial court held New Mexico law applied, which barred the action because Gagnon was not licensed. The court of appeals reversed, holding the law of Colorado applied, and rendered the contract enforceable.

ISSUE: Should an issue be resolved by applying the law of that state which has the "most significant relationship" to that issue?

HOLDING AND DECISION: (Hodges, C.J.) Yes. The approach taken by the Restatement (Second) of Conflict of Laws is to apply the law of that state having the "most significant relationship" to the issue at hand to resolve that issue. Section 196 thereof effectively creates a rebuttable presumption that the state where services are to be performed is the state having the most significant relationship to the issue of the validity of the contract. In this case, the presumption is valid and not rebutted. New Mexico is the state having the "most significant relationship." Its law barring actions by those not licensed there is designed to protect its citizens against substandard or hazardous construction and outweighs Colorado's interest in protecting the parties' contractual expectations. Thus, New Mexico law applies and bars this action on the contract. Reversed.

▌ ANALYSIS

Under the traditional conflict of laws rule, it was the law of the place of execution which governed issues relating to the formation of the contract. However, for issues relating to the performance of the contract, the law of the place of performance governed.

Quicknotes

ASSIGNOR A party who assigns his interest or rights to another.

CONSTRUCTION CONTRACT A contract containing provisions that specify the terms pursuant to which a building is to be constructed.

QUANTUM MERUIT Equitable doctrine allowing recovery for labor and materials provided by one party, even though no contract was entered into, in order to avoid unjust enrichment by the benefited party.

REBUTTABLE PRESUMPTION A rule of law, inferred from the existence of a particular set of facts, that is conclusive in the absence of contrary evidence.

Milkovich v. Saari

Injured passenger (P) v. Driver (D)

Minn. Sup. Ct., 295 Minn. 155, 203 N.W.2d 408 (1973).

NATURE OF CASE: Appeal from a denial of a motion to dismiss an action for damages for negligence.

FACT SUMMARY: Milkovich (P), a Canadian resident, was injured in Saari's (D) auto, when it crashed in Minnesota, a state which did not have a guest statute.

🏛 RULE OF LAW
To determine choice of law, a court should consider (1) predictability of results; (2) maintenance of interstate and international order; (3) simplification of a judicial task; (4) advancement of the forum's governmental interests; and (5) application of the better rule of law.

FACTS: Milkovich (P), a resident of Ontario, Canada, was a guest in the auto of Saari (D), also an Ontario resident, to shop and attend a play in Duluth. Saari (D) registered, garaged, and insured her car in Ontario, which has a guest statute. Milkovich (P) was injured when Saari's (D) car crashed in Minnesota, which did not have a guest statute. Milkovich (P) was hospitalized in Duluth for six weeks. She brought suit in Minnesota (as the Ontario guest statute required the guest to show gross negligence). The trial court denied Saari's (D) motion to dismiss, and she appealed.

ISSUE: To determine choice of law, should a court consider (1) predictability of results; (2) maintenance of interstate and international order; (3) simplification of a judicial task; (4) advancement of the forum's governmental interests; and (5) application of the better rule of law?

HOLDING AND DECISION: (Todd, J.) Yes. To determine choice of law, a court should consider (1) predictability of results; (2) maintenance of interstate and international order; (3) simplification of a judicial task; (4) advancement of the forum's governmental interest; and (5) application of the better rule of law. The rule of applying the law of the place of injury is out of date. Rather, a rule which looks to reason and justice should be adopted. Here, predictability of results is irrelevant to torts cases, but is more applicable to contracts cases generally, where persons agree to look to certain law. Simplification of the judicial task is not of much concern as either law could be applied here without difficulty. As for interstate and international relations, here the forum state has a substantial connection with the facts and issues by being the place of injury and hospitalization. What is compelling are advancements of the forum's governmental interests and application of the better rule of law. "While there may be more deterrent effect in our common-law rule of liability as opposed to the guest statute requirement of gross negligence, the main governmental interest involved is that of

any 'justice-administering state.'" The forum should not apply law inconsistent with its own concept of fairness and equity. As for the better rule of law, Minnesota's lack of a guest statute is the better approach. Guest statutes have lost favor as the collusive suits which they were designed to prevent can be easily uncovered. The motion was properly denied.

DISSENT: (Peterson, J.) The Canadian parties have concurred in the law of their province and, for them, American law should not be the better law. The approach used by the majority "is really little more than a mechanical application of the law of the forum."

▶ ANALYSIS

The rule of this case adopts the choice of law rule put forth by Professor Robert Leflar. This case has received criticism. Putting aside the tendency of courts to argue that their own law is the better law, this case seems to cast aside a strong interest which the province of Ontario would have had in the action. The car trip began and was to end in Ontario, the parties were residents of Ontario, and it appeared that Milkovich (P) was forum shopping as her original suit was filed first in Ontario. Also, the expectations of the Canadian insurer of Saari (D) were based on Ontario law. As for the better law problem, Professor Leflar admits that judges usually apply the law of the forum, but that they should be mature about the problem in making an impartial choice.

■━■

Quicknotes

FORUM-SHOPPING Refers to a situation in which one party to an action seeks to have the matter heard and determined by a court, or in a jurisdiction, that will provide it with the most favorable result.

GUEST STATUTE A state statute requiring a specified level of culpability, usually more than mere negligence, on the part of the driver of an automobile in order to be liable for injuries resulting to a gratuitous passenger.

■━■

Jepson v. General Casualty Co. of Wisconsin

Insured (P) v. Insurer (D)

Minn. Sup. Ct., 513 N.W.2d 467 (1994).

NATURE OF CASE: Appeal from declaratory judgment applying Minnesota law for insurance damages.

FACT SUMMARY: Jepson (P), who lived in Minnesota near the North Dakota border and purchased auto insurance through an agent in Minnesota, was injured in an accident in Arizona and then sought to benefit from Minnesota law, which permitted stacking of benefits, while North Dakota did not.

🏛 RULE OF LAW
In determining choice of law rules, predictability of result, maintenance of interstate and international order, simplification of the judicial task, advancement of the forum's governmental interest, and application of the better rule of law must be considered.

FACTS: Jepson (P) was injured while a passenger in a real estate agent's car in Arizona. At the time, he resided in Minnesota and had purchased auto insurance through a Minnesota agency, but had paid North Dakota rates, which were lower. After settling with the driver of the other car, Jepson (P) sought additional benefits under an insurance policy his North Dakota business had purchased from General Casualty Co. of Wisconsin (D) and which covered seven vehicles. The lower courts applied Minnesota law, which permitted stacking of benefits, while North Dakota law did not.

ISSUE: In determining choice of law rules, must predictability of result, maintenance of interstate and international order, simplification of the judicial task, advancement of the forum's governmental interest, and application of the better rule of law be considered?

HOLDING AND DECISION: (Page, J.) Yes. In determining choice of law rules, predictability of result, maintenance of interstate and international order, simplification of the judicial task, advancement of the forum's governmental interest, and application of the better rule of law must be considered. There is evidence Jepson (P) was forum shopping in bringing suit in Minnesota after securing no fault benefits payable under North Dakota law. Unlike the trial court and court of appeal, we find that the maintenance of interstate order weighs heavily in favor of applying North Dakota law. Because we do not find either stacking or anti-stacking to be a better rule, that consideration did not influence our choice of law. North Dakota law applies to Jepson's (P) stacking claim. So deciding how many vehicles may be stacked under the policy is moot. Reversed.

▶ ANALYSIS

The court held that forum law need not always be the better rule. Otherwise, consideration of that factor would be meaningless. The better rule should be the rule that makes good socioeconomic sense for the time when the court speaks.

■=■

Quicknotes

FORUM-SHOPPING Refers to a situation in which one party to an action seeks to have the matter heard and determined by a court, or in a jurisdiction, that will provide it with the most favorable result.

■=■

Pfau v. Trent Aluminum Co.

Injured passenger v. Driver

N.J. Sup. Ct., 55 N.J. 511, 263 A.2d 129 (1970).

NATURE OF CASE: Review of order reversing order striking an affirmative defense in a personal injury action.

FACT SUMMARY: Trent Aluminum (D), sued for personal injury, contended that a foreign state's choice-of-law rule should be applied if its substantive law were to be applied.

🏛 RULE OF LAW
A state's substantive law may be applied without its choice-of-law rules also being applied.

FACTS: Pfau (P) and Trent (D) were schoolmates at college in Iowa. Trent (D) was a New Jersey citizen and Pfau (P) a Connecticut citizen. While driving a vehicle belonging to his father's company, Trent Aluminum Co. (D), Trent (D) was involved in an auto accident in Iowa. Pfau (P) was a passenger in the vehicle. Trent Aluminum (D) contended that Iowa's guest statute applied, and raised this defense. Pfau (P) successfully moved to strike the defense, the court ruling Connecticut law, which contained no guest statute to be applicable. The court of appeals reversed, holding Connecticut's choice-of-law rule also to apply. Since Connecticut applied the lex loci rule, the court held Iowa law applicable. The New Jersey Supreme Court granted review.

ISSUE: May a state's substantive law be applied without its choice-of-law rules also being applied?

HOLDING AND DECISION: (Proctor, J.) Yes. A state's substantive law may be applied without its choice-of-law rules also being applied. Choice-of-law analysis is based on governmental interests, and a nonforum state's choice-of-law rule does not relate to its substantive interests in a litigation. This is particularly true when a state adheres to the lex loci rule, which has nothing at all to do with governmental interests. Consequently, applying Connecticut's choice-of-law rule would not promote any of its governmental interests in this litigation and should not be applied. [The court went on to hold that since Connecticut and New Jersey had identical law on the guest statute issue, there was no conflict to resolve.] Reversed and the order of the trial court reinstated.

▌ *ANALYSIS*

Some commentators have not taken the position apparently held here that choice-of-law rules are not relevant in a governmental interest analysis. Some have held, for instance, that choice-of-law rules can illustrate precisely what a state's governmental interests might be, as such interests are likely to be incorporated into choice-of-law rules. This debate has largely been theoretical; as a practical matter, a forum state's choice-of-law rules are almost always used.

■═■

Quicknotes

AFFIRMATIVE DEFENSE A manner of defending oneself against a claim not by denying the truth of the charge but by the introduction of some evidence challenging the plaintiff's right to bring the claim.

GUEST STATUTE A state statute requiring a specified level of culpability, usually more than mere negligence, on the part of the driver of an automobile in order to be liable for injuries resulting to a gratuitous passenger.

LEX LOCI DELICTI Refers to the location in which the unlawful activity giving rise to liability occurred.

RENVOI A doctrine pursuant to which a court adopts the conflict of law rules of a foreign jurisdiction, which requires the court to apply to the laws of its own forum.

■═■

Paul v. National Life

Deceased passenger's estate v. Deceased driver

W. Va. Sup. Ct. App., 177 W. Va. 427, 352 S.E.2d 550 (1986).

NATURE OF CASE: Appeal from dismissal of action for damages for wrongful death.

FACT SUMMARY: Paul's survivors (P) contended that the lex loci delicti rule for choice of law should be rejected.

🏛 RULE OF LAW
The lex loci delicti rule for choice of law should be applied, except when to do so would violate state public policy.

FACTS: Vickers, while driving her vehicle in Indiana, lost control and ran off the road. She and Paul, her passenger, were both killed. Both had been West Virginia residents. A wrongful death action was brought by Paul's survivors (P). The court applied Indiana's guest statute and dismissed. An appeal was taken, Paul's survivors (P) contending that the lex loci delicti rule for choice of law should not be followed.

ISSUE: Should the lex loci delicti rule for choice of law be applied, except when to do so would violate state public policy?

HOLDING AND DECISION: (Neely, J.) Yes. The lex loci delicti rule for choice of law should be applied, except when to do so would violate state public policy. In the last 30 years, this rule has been replaced in most states by a rather complicated analysis involving competing state interests. However, a reading of the relevant cases shows that the lex loci rule was discarded mostly to avoid unjust results in particular cases. The better approach is to retain the lex loci rule but simply not employ it in a particular situation when doing so would violate state public policy. The lex loci rule has the advantage of predictability, which helps to expedite cases. [The court went on to hold application of Indiana's guest statute to violate West Virginia public policy.] Vacated and remanded.

▶ ANALYSIS

Most of the landmark cases jettisoning the lex loci rule were decided between 1963 and 1973 and involved laws which the forum courts found distasteful. Guest statutes and interspousal immunity were the usual situations. Interestingly, in the intervening years, most states have abolished these doctrines, so the reasons for the departure from the lex loci rule largely no longer exist.

■=■

Quicknotes

GUEST STATUTE A state statute requiring a specified level of culpability, usually more than mere negligence, on the part of the driver of an automobile in order to be liable for injuries resulting to a gratuitous passenger.

LEX LOCI DELICTI Refers to the location in which the unlawful activity giving rise to liability occurred.

PUBLIC POLICY Policy administered by the state with respect to the health, safety and morals of its people in accordance with common notions of fairness and decency.

WRONGFUL DEATH An action brought by the beneficiaries of a deceased person, claiming that the deceased's death was the result of wrongful conduct by the defendant.

■=■

In re Air Crash Disaster Near Chicago, Illinois on May 25, 1979

Employees (P) v. Employer (D)

644 F.2d 594 (7th Cir. 1981).

NATURE OF CASE: Appeal from denial of defendant's motion to strike punitive damages awards in wrongful death actions.

FACT SUMMARY: Following the crash of a DC-10 jet airplane built by McDonnell Douglas Corporation (MDC) (D), the relatives of the deceased passengers were awarded punitive damages, as well as compensatory damages, in suits alleging wrongful death.

🏛 RULE OF LAW
In applying choice of law rules, dépeçage, the process of applying rules of different states on the basis of the precise issue involved, is appropriate.

FACTS: Following the air crash near Chicago, relatives of the 271 passengers who died were awarded compensatory and punitive damages, based on choice of law rules where the actions had originally been filed. MDC (D) and American Airlines (D) moved to strike the claims of punitive damages. The court allowed the motions to strike punitive damages claims against American (D) but not against MDC (D). MDC (D) appealed.

ISSUE: In applying choice of law rules, is dépeçage, the process of applying rules of different states on the basis of the precise issue involved, appropriate?

HOLDING AND DECISION: (Sprecher, J.) Yes. In applying choice of law rules, dépeçage, the process of applying rules of different states on the basis of the precise issue involved, is appropriate. The application of choice of law rules is not a mechanical process. Each state's interest in the specific question of punitive damages must be examined. Here, Illinois, the place of the injury, does not allow damages, Missouri, MDC's (D) principal place of business, does allow punitive damages, but California, place of MDC's (D) conduct, does not. American Airlines (D) has two principal places of business; one allows punitive damages, while the other does not. For the actions filed in Illinois, the application of the most significant relationship test leads to the use of Illinois law since it was the place of the injury. California follows the comparative impairment approach to choice of law questions. California has a strong public policy against punitive damages for wrongful death. All the motions to strike should have been granted. Affirmed in part, reversed in part.

▶ ANALYSIS

The court considered the law of several states. In addition to Illinois, California and New York, the laws of Hawaii, Puerto Rico, and Michigan were considered. The court here agreed with the district court that federal regulations regarding tort liability should be enacted.

Quicknotes

COMPENSATORY DAMAGES Measure of damages necessary to compensate victim for actual injuries suffered.

PUNITIVE DAMAGES Damages exceeding the actual injury suffered for the purposes of punishment, deterrence and comfort to plaintiff.

WRONGFUL DEATH An action brought by the beneficiaries of a deceased person, claiming that the deceased's death was the result of wrongful conduct by the defendant.

LICRA et UEJF v. Yahoo! Inc.

Antiracist group (P) v. Internet service provider (D)

www.gyoza.com/lapres/html/yahen.html, Tribunal de Grande Instance de Paris, May 22, 2000.

NATURE OF CASE: Action for damages for internet site's violation of French penal law.

FACT SUMMARY: The French League Against Racism and Antisemitism (LICRA) and the Jewish Students' Union of France (UEJF) (P) sued Yahoo! Inc. (D) because its website, Yahoo.com, included an auction page offering Nazi relics and flags for sale, in contravention of French criminal law.

🏛 RULE OF LAW
Where a website points toward sites, pages or forums that would likely be considered criminal or an illegal nuisance, it must warn surfers, by a banner, prior to entry to the site, to interrupt visiting that site to avoid sanctions under French law.

FACTS: Yahoo! Inc. (D) operated the Yahoo.com website which was accessible in France. LICRA (P) sued to prevent the sale of Nazi memorabilia through a Yahoo (D) auction page, claiming the sale of Nazi objects constituted a violation of French law.

ISSUE: Where a website points toward sites, pages or forums that would likely be considered criminal or an illegal nuisance, must it warn surfers, by a banner, prior to entry to the site, to interrupt visiting that site to avoid sanctions under French law?

HOLDING AND DECISION: (Opinion delivered by the Chief Justice) Yes. Where a website points toward sites, pages or forums that would likely be considered criminal or an illegal nuisance, it must warn surfers, by a banner, prior to entry to the site, to interrupt visiting that site to avoid sanctions under French law. Yahoo (D) has two months to formulate proposals of technical measures likely to lead to settlement of this dispute. Damages awarded to LICRA and UEJF.

▌ ANALYSIS

Yahoo (D) claimed that it did not have the technological means to block access to specific websites. A panel of specialists was later appointed to investigate. A similar case in Germany involving illegal pornographic websites, ended when the German Parliament enacted legislation holding internet providers liable only if they were aware of the content and failed to use technically possible and reasonable means to block it.

Quicknotes

AUCTION A public sale accomplished by means of competitive bidding.

Yahoo! Inc. v. La Ligue Contre le Racisme et L'Antisemitisme

Internet service provider (D) v. Antiracist group (P)

169 F. Supp. 2d 1181 (N.D. Cal. 2001).

NATURE OF CASE: Motion to declare unenforceable a French judgment against a U.S. company for violation of French law.

FACT SUMMARY: [Facts not stated in casebook excerpt, but case is an appeal of the judgment by a French court in *LICRA et UEJF v. Yahoo! Inc.*, Casenote p. 39. Yahoo! appealed on grounds that compliance interfered with U.S. constitutional free speech guarantees.]

RULE OF LAW

Principles of comity do not require the United States to permit foreign regulation of speech by a United States resident within the United States on the basis that such speech can be accessed by Internet users in that nation.

FACTS: [Facts not stated in casebook excerpt, but case is an appeal of the judgment by a French court in *LICRA et UEJF v. Yahoo! Inc.*, Casenote p. 39. After that judgment, Yahoo! Inc. posted on Yahoo.fr a warning to French citizens that searches might lead them to items that violate French law. Yahoo! Inc. also prohibited the auctioning on its website of items that promoted racist groups, excepting government-issue stamps and coins, and establishing a more permissive stance on items of personal expressions, such as books or films. Yahoo! did not attempt to technologically prevent French citizens from accessing websites auctioning any item.]

ISSUE: Do principles of comity require the United States to permit foreign regulation of speech by a United States resident within the United States on the basis that such speech can be accessed by Internet users in that nation?

HOLDING AND DECISION: (Fogel, J.) No. Principles of comity do not require the United States to permit foreign regulation of speech by a United States resident within the United States on the basis that such speech can be accessed by Internet users in that nation. Comity is neither mere courtesy and good will, nor an absolute obligation. U.S. courts generally recognize foreign judgments as long as enforcement is not contrary to U.S. interests. Enforcement of the French order directing Yahoo! to prevent French citizens from accessing Nazi items offered for sale by third parties would violate Yahoo!'s first amendment rights, and therefore cannot be enforced.

▶ *ANALYSIS*

Consider the implications of a different result in this case. If other countries can block information on the Internet and impose their values and customs on the rest of the world,

the Internet would be reduced to disseminating the least and only the most generic information, which would severely restrict American rights to free speech.

Quicknotes

COMITY A rule pursuant to which courts in one state give deference to the statutes and judicial decisions of the courts of another state.

Choice of Law: The Constitution

Quick Reference Rules of Law

Home Ins. Co. v. Dick

Insurer (D) v. Insured (P)

281 U.S. 397 (1930).

NATURE OF CASE: Appeal from judgment for plaintiff in suit to recover proceeds of a fire insurance policy.

FACT SUMMARY: Dick (P) sued Home Insurance (D), a New York company, in Texas on a policy of fire insurance issued in Mexico on a boat located there. Suit was brought within the Texas statute of limitations but beyond the period specified in the insurance contract.

🏛 RULE OF LAW
A state may impose its laws and regulations to alter the terms of a contract sued upon in its courts only where the contract was entered into or was to be at least partially performed within the state.

FACTS: Dick (P), a citizen of Texas residing in Mexico, purchased a fire insurance policy in that country to cover a boat operated in Mexican waters. The policy was issued by a Mexican company which reinsured part of the risk to Home Insurance Co. (D), a New York company. The reinsurance agreement was executed in Mexico and New York. After loss of the boat by fire, Dick (P) brought suit in a Texas court to recover on the policy. The policy contained a clause requiring any such suit be brought within a year of the loss. A Texas statute required any such clause extend the time to sue to no less than two years. Dick (P) brought suit more than one year after the loss, but the Texas court applied the Texas statute to allow the suit to proceed.

ISSUE: Does application of its own laws by a state to alter the terms of a contract sued upon in its courts violate due process of law where the contract was neither entered into or to be partially performed within its borders?

HOLDING AND DECISION: (Brandeis, J.) Yes. The Texas statute is not merely a statute of limitations for it can, under proper circumstances, extend liability where none would exist by the terms of the contract. It is, however, immaterial whether the statute is looked upon as procedural or substantive or remedial. Texas had no connection either with the original policy or with the reinsurance contract save that Dick (P) was a citizen of the state and he brought suit in Texas courts. Where neither the contract itself or any of the parties were subject to Texas law at the time the contract was entered into or to be performed, Texas may not apply its law to alter the terms of that contract. To do so would violate the due process clause of the federal Constitution. Reversed.

▶ ANALYSIS

The application of the Due Process Clause in this case served notice that states were not free to make any choice of law to apply to a case in its courts. The minimum contacts approach is similar to that necessary to impose jurisdiction on an out-of-state party. To hold otherwise would be to encourage forum shopping by plaintiffs to find a favorable state.

■■■

Quicknotes

DUE PROCESS CLAUSE Clauses found in the Fifth and Fourteenth Amendments to the United States Constitution providing that no person shall be deprived of "life, liberty, or property, without due process of law."

FORUM-SHOPPING Refers to a situation in which one party to an action seeks to have the matter heard and determined by a court, or in a jurisdiction, that will provide it with the most favorable result.

MINIMUM CONTACTS The minimum degree of contact necessary in order to sustain a cause of action within a particular forum, consistent with the requirements of due process.

STATUTE OF LIMITATIONS A law prescribing the period in which a legal action may be commenced.

TEXAS REVISED CIVIL STATUTE, § 5545 Contracts may not include provisions that limit the time in which to sue to less than two years.

■■■

Bradford Electric Light Co. v. Clapper

Employer (D) v. Employee's wife (P)

286 U.S. 145 (1932).

NATURE OF CASE: Review of award of damages for wrongful death.

FACT SUMMARY: Bradford Electric Light Co. (D) contended that New Hampshire was bound to give effect to a defense existing under the law of Vermont, where both it and Clapper (P) were domiciled.

🏛 RULE OF LAW
When the litigants in a suit reside in a state different than the forum and that state provides a defense to the cause of action, the forum state must allow the defense to be raised.

FACTS: Clapper (P) was employed by Bradford Electric Light Co. (Bradford) (D); both parties were domiciled in Vermont. While working on a power line just over the state line in New Hampshire, Clapper was killed. Clapper's estate administrator (P) filed an action in New Hampshire. Bradford (D) attempted to raise the defense of exclusivity of workers' compensation as a defense available under Vermont law and expressly applicable extraterritorially. The trial court applied New Hampshire law, which did not provide for the exclusive remedy defense. A jury awarded $4,000, and Bradford (D) appealed, arguing that since both parties were domiciled in Vermont, Vermont's defense should have been applied. The Supreme Court granted review.

ISSUE: When the litigants in a suit reside in a state different than the forum and that state provides a defense to the cause of action, must the forum state allow the defense to be raised?

HOLDING AND DECISION: (Brandeis, J.) Yes. When the litigants in a suit reside in a state different than the forum and that state provides a defense to the cause of action, the forum state must allow the defense to be raised. The Full Faith and Credit Clause prohibits the forum state from granting a litigant therein rights greater than he would be given by the state of his domicile. To hold otherwise would gravely impair the ability of states to enact effective legislation, as such laws could be circumvented by bringing lawsuits elsewhere. Consequently, when a state creates a defense to a suit and both parties in a litigation are citizens of that state, the forum must provide that defense, whether or not the forum's substantive law provides the defense. This is the case here. Reversed and remanded.

▶ ANALYSIS

The rule enunciated by the Court may not have been iron-clad. In a brief passage that could be characterized as dicta, the Court noted that the defense asserted did not violate New Hampshire public policy. The implication would appear to be that a defense that did so violate might not have to be allowed.

■=■

Quicknotes

DOMICILE A person's permanent home or principal establishment to which he has an intention of returning when he is absent therefrom.

FULL FAITH AND CREDIT Doctrine that a judgment by a court of one state shall be given the same effect in another state.

PUBLIC POLICY Policy administered by the state with respect to the health, safety and morals of its people in accordance with common notions of fairness and decency.

WORKERS' COMPENSATION Fixed awards provided to employees for job-related injuries.

WRONGFUL DEATH An action brought by the beneficiaries of a deceased person, claiming that the deceased's death was the result of wrongful conduct by the defendant.

■=■

Alaska Packers Assoc. v. Industrial Acc. Comm'n

Fish packer (D) v. State agency (P)

294 U.S. 532 (1935).

NATURE OF CASE: Review of award of workers' compensation benefits.

FACT SUMMARY: California's provision bringing under its workers' compensation law employment contracts executed in the state was challenged as violating the Full Faith and Credit Clause when applied to an extraterritorial accident suffered by a nonresident alien, Palma (P).

RULE OF LAW
A forum state may give effect to its own state's law over that of the place of accident if the extraterritorial law violates the public policy of the forum state.

FACTS: Palma (P), a nonresident alien, contracted with Alaska Packers Association (D), an Alaska organization, to work in Alaska. The contract was made in San Francisco and stated that the parties stipulated to be bound by Alaska's workers' compensation law. Palma (P), while working in Alaska, was injured there. After completing the contract and returning to California, he applied for workers' compensation there. As California law brought within the ambit of workers' compensation all employment agreements made in California, the California Industrial Accident Commission (P), ruling that Alaska's law could not be asserted as a defense to Palma's (P) claim, awarded him compensation. The Association (D) appealed, arguing that Alaska law should have been applied under the Full Faith and Credit Clause. The California Supreme Court affirmed, and the U.S. Supreme Court granted review.

ISSUE: May a forum state give effect to its own state's law over that of the place of accident if such extraterritorial law violates the public policy of the forum state?

HOLDING AND DECISION: (Stone, J.) Yes. A forum state may give effect to its own state's law over that of the place of accident if such extraterritorial law violates the public policy of the forum state. Taken literally, the Full Faith and Credit Clause would require a state to always give effect to a foreign law which competed with a local law under all circumstances. This would lead to the absurd result of each state always giving effect to a law other than its own, i.e., the law of the place of the injury would only be enforced in a foreign jurisdiction. The Clause cannot be construed to have this effect. Rather, the proper analysis is to look at the competing laws, and to consider whether the extraterritorial law embodies a policy of the enacting state strong enough to override the presumption that a forum state's court may enforce the laws of that state. Certainly, when enforcing the law of another state would violate public policy of the forum state, the Clause does not require the

forum law to be enforced. Here, California's stated policy is to see a broad application of its workers' compensation law, and not to apply California law would violate this policy. No rational basis was put forth for denying the California courts the right to apply their own state's laws. Affirmed.

ANALYSIS

The Court also rejected the argument that application of California law here would be a violation of due process, concluding that the California law, as applied, did not lack a rational basis or involve any arbitrary or unreasonable exercise of state power. This case presaged the "center of gravity" test for conflicts law, which in recent times has supplanted the lex loci delicti law as the most generally accepted approach to resolving conflicts in tort cases. The approach urged by the Alaska Packers Association (D) would have amounted to a constitutionalization of the lex loci rule, which the Court was not inclined to do.

▪══▪

Quicknotes

CALIFORNIA WORKMEN'S COMPENSATION ACT, § 27(a) No employment contract or regulation can exempt employers from liability for the compensation set by this act.

CAL. W.C.A., § 58 Provides for jurisdiction over all controversies arising out of injuries suffered outside the state by California residents hired in California.

FULL FAITH AND CREDIT CLAUSE State judicial proceedings shall have such faith and credit given them in every court in the United States as they would in their own state.

PUBLIC POLICY Policy administered by the state with respect to the health, safety and morals of its people in accordance with common notions of fairness and decency.

▪══▪

Pacific Employers Ins. Co. v. Industrial Acc. Comm'n

California insurer (P) v. Massachusetts agency (D)

306 U.S. 493 (1939).

NATURE OF CASE: Appeal from award of workmen's compensation benefits.

FACT SUMMARY: The claimant was a Massachusetts employee of a Massachusetts employer who was injured while on the job in California. He filed a claim for benefits under the California Workmen's Compensation Act.

🏛 RULE OF LAW
The full faith and credit doctrine may not be invoked where the strong public policy of the forum state would find the enforcement of another state's statutes obnoxious.

FACTS: While in California on company business, a Massachusetts employee of a Massachusetts employer was injured in the course of his duties. He filed a claim for benefits under the California Workmen's Compensation Act and was granted the benefits provided by the California Act. The Industrial Accident Commission of California (P) directed that the claimant's benefits be paid by Pacific Employers Insurance Co. (D), the employer's insurance carrier. The company contended that benefits should be awarded on the basis of benefits provided by the Massachusetts workmen's compensation laws, since the contract of employment was entered into in Massachusetts. The Massachusetts statutes setting forth the jurisdiction over compensable injuries stated that the employee waived his rights to recover under the laws of another state unless he specifically gave written notice of an election not to waive. The claimant gave no such notice. The applicable California statute provided that California would have exclusive jurisdiction over accidents occurring within the state. Both statutes gave the respective states jurisdiction over injuries outside the state where the contract of hire was entered into within the state. Pacific Employers (D) contended that the Full Faith and Credit Clause required California to recognize the provisions of the Massachusetts Act.

ISSUE: Does the Full Faith and Credit Clause require a forum state to enforce the laws of another state despite a strong public policy in the forum state to control accidents within its borders?

HOLDING AND DECISION: (Stone, J.) No. The Massachusetts statutes vesting jurisdiction in that state over accidents occurring within that state under a contract of hire entered into in Massachusetts is certainly constitutional. The same may be said of the similar California provisions. Each state could voluntarily opt to enforce the statutes of the other in appropriate circumstances. Each state has a valid interest in

providing for the welfare of its own employees injured within the state and may provide for the compensation of employees temporarily out of the state. But to force California to enforce the Massachusetts provisions would be to deny to California the right to give effect to the strong public policy of that state rightfully translated into law. The employee was injured in California, his benefits are payable there, and any medical bills or other attendant expenses will be incurred there. To enforce full faith and credit would be to deny to California the right to apply its own remedy and it would be administratively difficult, if not impossible, to provide the claimant his remedies provided by Massachusetts. This would leave the claimant without a viable remedy for his injuries. The Full Faith and Credit Clause does not empower one state to legislate for another or to project its own laws across state lines where, to do so, would offend the public policy of the other state. Affirmed.

▶ ANALYSIS

This case is an example of the development of choice of law rules in rejection of the vested rights doctrine. While couched in a full faith and credit context, the real issue in this case was choice of law and due process. The Supreme Court has generally followed the policy of enforcing full faith and credit only in those situations where the state having jurisdiction over the parties has asserted its law. This case represents a choice of laws analysis based on the most significant contact theory. Under this theory, the court looks at the conduct of the parties and the location where that conduct occurred. The court then determines which activities are relevant to the issues of the lawsuit and where those relevant activities occurred. The state in which the most number of significant or relevant contacts were made concerning the transaction is deemed to have the most appropriate law to apply. While this approach might appear to be somewhat mechanical, in operation it becomes rather discretionary. The determination of which activities are significant is not a scientific process. Further, the court may decide that one significant contact is more relevant than another. In this case, the place of contracting for the employment was a significant contact with Massachusetts. But the California court found that the place of contracting had little relevance and, consequently, gave that contact little weight in its decision. Critics of this approach have pointed to this as a defect in the application of the significant contact approach. They argue that while the contact analysis may be a more realistic approach to choice of laws than was the vested right doctrine, the wide discretion

Continued on next page.

given to the court leads to a loss of uniformity and predict-ability of result.

■≡■

Quicknotes

FULL FAITH AND CREDIT Doctrine that a judgment by a court of one state shall be given the same effect in another state.

WORKERS' COMPENSATION ACT A statute making the employer strictly liable to an employee for injuries sustained by the employee in the course of employment. The compensation scheduled under the Act is an exclusive remedy, barring any common-law remedy which the employee may have had.

■≡■

Allstate Ins. Co. v. Hague

Insurance company (D) v. Wife of deceased motorist (P)

449 U.S. 302 (1981).

NATURE OF CASE: Appeal from award of insurance proceeds.

FACT SUMMARY: Allstate (D) contended that the Minnesota state courts should have applied the laws of the state of Wisconsin at a personal injury trial.

🏛 RULE OF LAW
If a state has only insignificant contact with the parties and the occurrence or transaction, application of its law is unconstitutional.

FACTS: Hague's (P) late husband, Ralph Hague, died of injuries suffered when a motorcycle on which he was a passenger was struck from behind by an automobile in Pierce County, Wisconsin. The operators of both vehicles, and Hague, were residents of Wisconsin. Hague worked in Red Wing, Minnesota, and commuted to work from Wisconsin. After the accident, Mrs. Hague (P) moved to Red Wing and established residence in Minnesota. She then filed suit in Minnesota District Court against Allstate (D), which had issued an automobile insurance for Mr. Hague, asking that Minnesota law be applied so that she could "stack" the uninsured motorist coverage on each of her late husband's three automobiles, to provide for a larger recovery. The Minnesota Supreme Court affirmed a summary judgment for Hague (P), which held that Minnesota's choice of law rules required the application of Minnesota law permitting stacking. Allstate (D) then appealed.

ISSUE: If a state has only an insignificant contact with the parties and the occurrence or transaction, is the application of its law unconstitutional?

HOLDING AND DECISION: (Brennan, J.) Yes. If a state has only an insignificant contact with the parties and the occurrence or transaction, application of its law is unconstitutional. For a state's substantive law to be selected in a constitutionally permissible manner, the state must have a significant contact or significant aggregation of contacts, creating state interests, such that choice of its law is neither arbitrary nor fundamentally unfair. Here, Mr. Hague was a member of Minnesota's work force; he commuted to work in Minnesota; and Allstate's (D) presence in Minnesota gave Minnesota an interest in regulating the company's insurance obligations insofar as they affected both a Minnesota resident and court-appointed representative, Mrs. Hague (P), and a long-standing member of Minnesota's work force, Mr. Hague. Affirmed.

CONCURRENCE: (Stevens, J.) Allstate (D) has failed to establish that Minnesota's refusal to apply Wisconsin law poses any direct or indirect threat to Wisconsin's sovereignty.

The decision of the Minnesota courts does not frustrate the reasonable expectations of the contracting parties.

DISSENT: (Powell, J.) The contacts between Minnesota and this litigation are either trivial or irrelevant to the furthering of any public policy in Minnesota.

▶ ANALYSIS

In a lower court decision commenting on this case, the court stated that the significant contacts analysis in this case "addresses the traditional concerns of due process, i.e., preventing unfairness to the parties and promoting interstate relations." See *McCluney v. Jos. Schlitz Brewing Co.*, 649 F.2d 578 (8th Cir. 1981).

■=■

Quicknotes

DUE PROCESS The constitutional mandate requiring the courts to protect and enforce individuals' rights and liberties consistent with prevailing principles of fairness and justice and prohibiting the federal and state governments from such activities that deprive its citizens of a life, liberty or property interest.

FULL FAITH AND CREDIT ACT State judicial proceedings shall have such faith and credit given them in every court in the United States as they would in their own state.

MINIMUM CONTACTS The minimum degree of contact necessary in order to sustain a cause of action within a particular forum, consistent with the requirements of due process.

SUMMARY JUDGMENT Judgment rendered by a court in response to a motion by one of the parties, claiming that the lack of a question of material fact in respect to an issue warrants disposition of the issue without consideration by the jury.

■=■

Phillips Petroleum Co. v. Shutts

Natural gas producer (D) v. Landowner (P)

472 U.S. 797 (1985).

NATURE OF CASE: Appeal from award of interest on royalty payments.

FACT SUMMARY: Phillips (D) contended the trial court erred in applying Kansas law to Shutts's (P) class claim for interest on royalty payments.

🏛 RULE OF LAW
In a class action involving plaintiffs from several states, the application of one state's substantive law rests upon whether that state has significant contact and interest such that the choice of its law is neither arbitrary nor fundamentally unfair.

FACTS: Phillips (D), a Delaware corporation with a principal place of business in Oklahoma, leased land in 11 states from Shutts (P) and others similarly situated. A class action was brought to recover interest on royalties arising under the lease agreements. The suit was brought in Kansas and the trial court applied Kansas law. Phillips (D) appealed, contending the application of Kansas law violated due process. The Kansas court of last resort affirmed. The Supreme Court granted certiorari.

ISSUE: Does the application of state substantive law rest upon whether that state has significant contact and interest such that the choice of its law is neither arbitrary nor fundamentally unfair?

HOLDING AND DECISION: (Rehnquist, J.) Yes. In a class action involving parties from several states, the application of one state's substantive law rests upon whether that state has significant contact and interest such that such application is not arbitrary or fundamentally unfair. In this case, 99% of the leases and 97% of the plaintiffs had no contact with Kansas. Further, there was no common fund in Kansas. Thus the application of that state's law was arbitrary and fundamentally unfair. Affirmed and remanded.

CONCURRENCE AND DISSENT: (Stevens, J.) The Court was correct in holding Kansas had jurisdiction over the action, yet because of the parties' expectations, Kansas law should have applied.

▌ *ANALYSIS*

The Court points out that the determination of jurisdiction over the defendant and the application of choice of law principles are distinct inquiries. The constitutional limitations on choice of law determinations are not altered by how burdensome it would be to apply a particular state law. This of course is not the case in a jurisdictional inquiry.

■■■

Quicknotes

CERTIORARI A discretionary writ issued by a superior court to an inferior court in order to review the lower court's decisions; the Supreme Court's writ ordering such review.

CLASS ACTION A suit commenced by a representative on behalf of an ascertainable group that is too large to appear in court, who shares a commonality of interests and who will benefit from a successful result.

FULL FAITH AND CREDIT CLAUSE State judicial proceedings shall have such faith and credit given them in every court in the United States as they would in their own state.

■■■

Hughes v. Fetter

Estate of deceased motorist (P) v. Other motorist (D)

341 U.S. 609 (1951).

NATURE OF CASE: Wrongful death suit.

FACT SUMMARY: Hughes (P), a resident of Illinois, was killed in an auto accident in that state by Fetter (D), a resident of Wisconsin. Hughes's (P) administrator brought a wrongful death suit against Fetter (D) in Wisconsin, although Wisconsin law precluded such suits for deaths outside Wisconsin.

🏛 RULE OF LAW
While the Full Faith and Credit Clause does not require the forum state to give force to a sister state's law that conflicts with its own public policy, the forum state cannot deny recovery merely because the act giving rise to the lawsuit occurred outside its borders.

FACTS: While Fetter (D) was driving in Illinois, he was involved in an auto accident with Hughes (P). Fetter (D) was a resident of Wisconsin, and Hughes (P), who was killed, was a resident of Illinois. Both states had wrongful death statutes, and Hughes's (P) administrator brought suit against Fetter (D) in Wisconsin. The suit was dismissed on the ground that the Wisconsin wrongful death statute precluded recovery where the death occurred outside Wisconsin.

ISSUE: May the forum state be required by the Full Faith and Credit Clause to give force to a sister state's law that conflicts with its own public policy?

HOLDING AND DECISION: (Black, J.) No. In this case, however, there is no real conflict. Wisconsin recognizes the wrongful death action, as does Illinois. The only reason for excluding this suit is that the death occurred in Illinois. Since both the defendant individual and the defendant insurance company are domiciled in Wisconsin, there is sufficient contact for Wisconsin to provide a forum. The exclusion cannot be justified on a blanket statutory policy of "forum non conveniens" since in many circumstances Wisconsin might be the only state where jurisdiction could be had over the defendant. While true conflicts in public policies between states must be arbitrated by this court, Wisconsin has no public policy against this type of suit. Reversed and remanded.

DISSENT: (Frankfurter, J.) Since service of process could be had by substituted service in Illinois and were the circumstances reversed Illinois would refuse jurisdiction, there is no compelling reason to force Wisconsin to enforce Illinois law in its courts.

▶ ANALYSIS

Some commentators have felt this case was decided on Fourteenth Amendment equal protection grounds, rather than Full Faith and Credit. Application of the similar law in Illinois was later denied enforcement in another suit involving an airplane crash in Utah. The decision was rested on the same arguments as the principal case. Individual cases of "forum non conveniens" dismissals have been upheld where the facts supported the decision.

Quicknotes

FORUM NON CONVENIENS An equitable doctrine permitting a court to refrain from hearing and determining a case when the matter may be more properly and fairly heard in another forum.

FULL FAITH AND CREDIT CLAUSE State judicial proceedings shall have such faith and credit given them in every court in the United States as they would in their own state.

NEGLIGENCE Conduct falling below the standard of care that a reasonable person would demonstrate under similar conditions.

WRONGFUL DEATH An action brought by the beneficiaries of a deceased person, claiming that the deceased's death was the result of wrongful conduct by the defendant.

Tennessee Coal, Iron & R.R. Co. v. George

Railroad company (D) v. Engineer (P)

233 U.S. 354 (1914).

NATURE OF CASE: Suit for work-related personal injuries.

FACT SUMMARY: George (P) was injured on the job while employed by Tennessee Coal, Iron & R.R. Co. (D) in Alabama. He brought suit in Georgia under an Alabama statute holding the employer liable for injuries caused by defective equipment.

RULE OF LAW
A transitory cause of action can be maintained in another state, even though the statute creating the cause of action provides that the action must be maintained in local domestic courts.

FACTS: George (P) was employed by Tennessee Coal, Iron & R.R. Co. (D) in Alabama as an engineer. He was injured when a defective locomotive throttle caused the locomotive to run over him. Alabama has a statute which provides that an employer is liable for injuries to an employee caused by defective equipment. This statute abrogated the common law defenses of an employer. George (P) brought suit in Georgia under this statute, but Tennessee Coal (D) moved to dismiss on the grounds that the Alabama statute required suits under it to be brought in Alabama courts only. Judgment was entered for George (P) and affirmed on appeal. The Supreme Court granted certiorari.

ISSUE: Where a transitory cause of action is created by statute, will the requirement that actions under the statute be brought only in local courts be enforceable when the suit is brought elsewhere?

HOLDING AND DECISION: (Lamar, J.) No. While the statute creating this cause of action also restricted suits under it to Alabama courts, the cause of action is, by the terms of the statute, transitory. This is not a case where the right and the remedy are so united that the remedy cannot be enforced except by a specific court. The statute allows any court in Alabama to hear this type of suit. But if either the defendant or the plaintiff has moved since the accident, an Alabama court may not be the best venue. So long as Georgia is capable of trying the case according to the Alabama statute, full faith and credit requires she do so. Since Georgia was able to try the case, the judgment in favor of George (P) is affirmed.

ANALYSIS

Some variations on the circumstances in the principal case have occurred where a wrongful death suit is brought in one state based on the wrongful death statute of a sister state. It has been held that the forum state must recognize the cause of action but need not recognize a maximum recovery limit imposed by the same statute. This has been justified on the basis that the right created is substantive, while the recovery limit is procedural and procedural matters are not entitled to full faith and credit enforcement.

■■■■

Quicknotes

ALABAMA CODE, § 3910 Master is liable to employee for injuries caused by machinery defect.

ALABAMA CODE, § 6115 Actions under § 3910 must be brought in an Alabama court.

CERTIORARI A discretionary writ issued by a superior court to an inferior court in order to review the lower court's decisions; the Supreme Court's writ ordering such review.

FULL FAITH AND CREDIT CLAUSE State judicial proceedings shall have such faith and credit given them in every court in the United States as they would in their own state.

■■■■

Supreme Court of N.H. v. Piper

State (P) v. Bar applicant (D)

470 U.S. 274 (1985).

NATURE OF CASE: Appeal of an invalidation of state bar residency requirement.

FACT SUMMARY: Piper (P), a Vermont resident, was denied permission to apply to the New Hampshire bar due to her nonresidency.

🏛 RULE OF LAW
A state may not disqualify a bar applicant because of nonresidency.

FACTS: Piper (P) resided in Vermont, about 1/4 mile away from New Hampshire. Piper (P) applied to the New Hampshire bar. She was rejected because of a court rule mandating a residency requirement on bar members. Piper (P) challenged this as a violation of the Privileges and Immunities Clause of Article IV, § 2. The court of appeals held the residency requirement unconstitutional. The New Hampshire Supreme Court appealed.

ISSUE: May a state disqualify a bar applicant because of nonresidency?

HOLDING AND DECISION: (Powell, J.) No. A state may not disqualify a bar applicant because of non-residency. An article IV, § 2 privileges and immunities analysis requires two steps. The first question is whether the right asserted is a privilege or immunity within the scope of the clause. The right to livelihood has long been so considered. The practice of law is an important part of the national economy, and is important to the securing of rights. While an attorney is an officer of the court, his duties are not so bound up with the state that his office should be considered a state function. Therefore, the clause applies. The second question is whether state deprivation bears a substantial relationship to a legitimate objective. The state's justifications here include guaranteeing familiarity with local rules, maintaining discipline, ensuring availability, and encouraging pro bono work. However, none of these goals appears to this Court to be significantly advanced by the challenged rule. Therefore, the Privileges and Immunities Clause of Article IV, § 2 bars the challenged rule. Affirmed.

▶ ANALYSIS

By no means are all state rights and privileges protected by the clause. The Court has construed the clause to apply to those rights of a citizen as a citizen bearing on the vitality of the nation as a cohesive entity. The right to livelihood falls within this.

Quicknotes

PRO BONO Services rendered without charge.

PRIVILEGES AND IMMUNITIES CLAUSE Refers to the guarantee set forth in the Fourteenth Amendment to the United States Constitution recognizing that any individual born in any of the United States is entitled to both state and national citizenship and guaranteeing such citizens the privileges and immunities thereof.

Jurisdiction of Courts

Quick Reference Rules of Law

World-Wide Volkswagen Corp. v. Woodson

Car seller (D) v. Car buyer (P)

444 U.S. 286 (1980).

NATURE OF CASE: Appeal from rejection of challenge to in personam jurisdiction in a products liability action brought by Robinson.

FACT SUMMARY: World-Wide Volkswagen (WWV) (P) challenged an Oklahoma district court's (D) in personam jurisdiction in a products liability action brought by Robinson on the grounds that World-Wide Volkswagen's (P) only contacts with Oklahoma was that Robinson bought a World-Wide Volkswagen (P) car in New York and drove it through Oklahoma.

RULE OF LAW
A state court may exercise personal jurisdiction over a nonresident defendant only so long as there exists minimum contacts between the defendant and the forum state.

FACTS: Robinson bought a World-Wide Volkswagen (WWV) (P) car in New York. En route to Arizona, Robinson got into an automobile accident in Oklahoma and brought a products liability action against WWV (P) in Oklahoma. WWV (P) was incorporated and had its business in New York. WWV (P) distributed vehicles, parts, and accessories, under contract with Volkswagen, to retail dealers in New York, New Jersey, and Connecticut. WWV (P) did no business in Oklahoma, had no agents in Oklahoma, did not advertise in Oklahoma, nor use any media in Oklahoma. WWV (P) challenged the Oklahoma court's (D) in personam jurisdiction over WWV (P) on the grounds that WWV (P) had no minimum contacts with Oklahoma. The district court (D) rejected WWV's (P) challenge, as did the Oklahoma Supreme Court. WWV (P) appealed to the United States Supreme Court.

ISSUE: May a state court exercise personal jurisdiction over a nonresident defendant only so long as there exists minimum contacts between the defendant and the forum state?

HOLDING AND DECISION: (White, J.) Yes. A state court may exercise personal jurisdiction over a nonresident defendant only so long as there exists minimum contacts between the defendant and the forum state. This minimum contacts requirement serves two purposes: (1) It protects the defendant against the burdens of litigating in an inconvenient forum; and (2) It ensures that the states, through their courts, do not reach out beyond the limits imposed on them by their status as coequal sovereigns in a federal system. Additionally, the Due Process Clause, acting as an instrument of interstate federalism, may sometimes divest a state of its power to render a valid judgment. Here, WWV (P) did not have minimum contacts with Oklahoma. WWV's (P) only contact with the state was that one of its

cars had been driven through the state. It would be unreasonable to expect WWV (P) to foresee that an accident would occur in Oklahoma and have to defend actions wherever their cars are taken. This situation is distinguished from those where a nonresident corporation purposefully avails itself of the state's commerce by introducing a product to the state's market and can therefore fall within the state's in personam jurisdiction. In such a situation, the corporation can foresee that litigation might occur in the availed state. Here, however, WWV's (P) only contact with Oklahoma was that a consumer drove a car through the state. Because such a contact is insufficient to satisfy the minimal contacts requirement, the Oklahoma court (D) does not have in personam jurisdiction over WWV (P). Reversed.

DISSENT: (Brennan, J.) WWV's (P) contacts to Oklahoma were strong in that the accident occurred in the state, witnesses lived in the state, and the state has a legitimate interest in preserving its interstate highways. The sale of automobiles presupposes that such cars will be driven to distant states. This is tantamount to introducing a product into the market of a state and the likelihood of litigation in other states is foreseeable. Therefore, WWV (P) had sufficient contacts with Oklahoma for jurisdiction to apply.

▶ ANALYSIS

The minimum contacts test was originally established in *International Shoe Co. v. Washington*, 326 U.S. 310 (1945). The test is vague and always requires a detailed examination of the facts. Among the factors courts look at are manifest state interests, purposeful availment, foreseeability, fairness, and states' long-arm statutes.

Quicknotes

DUE PROCESS The constitutional mandate requiring the courts to protect and enforce individuals' rights and liberties consistent with prevailing principles of fairness and justice and prohibiting the federal and state governments from such activities that deprive its citizens of a life, liberty or property interest.

MINIMUM CONTACTS The minimum degree of contact necessary in order to sustain a cause of action within a particular forum, consistent with the requirements of due process.

PERSONAL JURISDICTION The court's authority over a person or parties to a lawsuit.

Asahi Metal Industry Co., Ltd. v. Superior Court

Japanese manufacturer (P) v. State court (D)

480 U.S. 102 (1987).

NATURE OF CASE: Appeal from discharge of writ quashing service of summons.

FACT SUMMARY: Asahi Metal Industry Co., Ltd. (P) appealed from a decision of the California Supreme Court discharging a peremptory writ issued by the appeals court quashing service of summons in Cheng Shin's indemnity action, contending that there did not exist minimum contacts between California and Asahi (P) sufficient to sustain jurisdiction.

🏛 RULE OF LAW
Minimum contacts sufficient to sustain jurisdiction are not satisfied simply by the placement of a product into the stream of commerce coupled with an awareness that its product would reach the forum state.

FACTS: Asahi Metal Industry Co., Ltd. (P), a Japanese corporation, manufactured tire valve assemblies in Japan, selling some of them to Cheng Shin, a Taiwanese company which incorporated them into the motorcycles it manufactured. Zurcher was seriously injured in a motorcycle accident, and a companion was killed. He sued Cheng Shin, alleging the motorcycle tire manufactured by Cheng Shin was defective. Cheng Shin sought indemnity from Asahi (P), and the main action settled. Asahi (P) moved to quash service of summons, contending that jurisdiction could not be maintained by California, the state in which Zurcher filed his action, consistent with the Due Process Clause of the Fourteenth Amendment. The evidence indicated that Asahi's (P) sales to Cheng Shin took place in Taiwan, and shipments went from Japan to Taiwan. Cheng Shin purchased valve assemblies from other manufacturers. Sales to Cheng Shin never amounted to more than 1.5% of Asahi's (P) income. Approximately 20% of Cheng Shin's sales in the United States are in California. In declaration, an attorney for Cheng Shin stated he made an informal examination of tires in a bike shop in Solano County, where Zurcher was injured, finding approximately 20% of the tires with Asahi's (P) trademark (25% of the tires manufactured by Cheng Shin). The Superior Court (D) denied the motion to quash, finding it reasonable that Asahi (P) defend its claim of defect in their product. The court of appeals issued a peremptory writ commanding the superior court (D) to quash service of summons. The state supreme court reversed and discharged the writ, finding that Asahi's (P) awareness that some of its product would reach California by placing it in the stream of commerce satisfied minimum contacts sufficient to sustain jurisdiction. From this decision, Asahi (P) appealed.

ISSUE: Are minimum contacts sufficient to sustain jurisdiction satisfied by the placement of a product into the stream of commerce, coupled with the awareness that its product would reach the forum state?

HOLDING AND DECISION: (O'Connor, J.) No. Minimum contacts sufficient to sustain jurisdiction are not satisfied by the placement of a product in the stream of commerce, coupled with the awareness that its product would reach the forum state. To satisfy minimum contacts, there must be some act by which the defendant purposefully avails itself of the privilege of conducting activities within the forum state. Although the courts that have squarely addressed this issue have been divided, the better view is that the defendant must do more than place a product in the stream of commerce. The unilateral act of a consumer bringing the product to the forum state is not sufficient. Asahi (P) has not purposefully availed itself of the California market. It does not do business in the state, conduct activities, maintain offices or agents, or advertise. Nor did it have anything to do with Cheng Shin's distribution system, which brought the tire valve assembly to California. Assertion of jurisdiction based on these facts exceeds the limits of due process. [The Court went on to consider the burden of defense on Asahi (P) and the slight interests of the state and Zurcher, finding the assertion of jurisdiction unreasonable and unfair.] Reversed.

CONCURRENCE: (Brennan, J.) The state supreme court correctly concluded that the stream of commerce theory, without more, has satisfied minimum contacts in most courts which have addressed the issue, and it has been preserved in the decision of this Court.

CONCURRENCE: (Stevens, J.) The minimum contacts analysis is unnecessary; the Court has found by weighing the appropriate factors that jurisdiction under these facts is unreasonable and unfair.

▶ *ANALYSIS*

The Brennan concurrence is quite on point in criticizing the plurality for its characterization of this case as involving the act of a consumer in bringing the product within the forum state. The argument presented in *World-Wide Volkswagen Corp. v. Woodson*, 444 U.S. 286 (1980), cited by the plurality, seems more applicable to distributors and retailers than to manufacturers of component parts.

■=■

Continued on next page.

Quicknotes

MINIMUM CONTACTS The minimum degree of contact necessary in order to sustain a cause of action within a particular forum, consistent with the requirements of due process.

Burger King Corp. v. Rudzewicz

Franchisor (P) v. Franchisee (D)

471 U.S. 462 (1985).

NATURE OF CASE: Appeal from denial of personal jurisdiction.

FACT SUMMARY: Rudzewicz (D) contended that the district court's exercise of personal jurisdiction over him violated due process.

🏛 RULE OF LAW
A choice of law provision in a contract may be considered in determining whether a defendant has purposely availed himself of the benefits and protections of the forum state such that it may exercise personal jurisdiction over him.

FACTS: Rudzewicz (D) and MacShara (D) applied for a Burger King (P) franchise in Michigan. Their application was accepted and a written agreement executed with the Burger King (P) corporate headquarters in Miami, Florida. The contract called for payments to be made to the Miami office, and that its terms would be interpreted and enforced under Florida law. Rudzewicz (D) and MacShara (D) defaulted on the payments, and Burger King (P) sued for breach in district court in Florida. The district court held it had both personal and subject matter jurisdiction over the defendants and entered judgment for Burger King (P). The court of appeals reversed, holding the choice of law provision was irrelevant to the determination of personal jurisdiction and excluded it in evaluating the contacts with Florida. Burger King (P) appealed.

ISSUE: Is a choice of law provision in a contract relevant to the determination of personal jurisdiction over a defendant?

HOLDING AND DECISION: (Brennan, J.) Yes. A choice of law provision in a contract may be considered in determining whether a defendant has purposely availed himself of the protection of the forum state such that it may exercise personal jurisdiction over him. While not dispositive, this element may be used to show the defendant's consent to abide by and avail himself of the laws of the state. Thus, the provision requiring application of Florida law, when considered with the other evidence of contacts, could be sufficient to allow personal jurisdiction over Rudzewicz (D). Reversed.

DISSENT: (Stevens, J.) Rudzewicz (D) had no reason to believe he would be subject to suit anywhere but in Michigan. All of the negotiations with Burger King (P) were in Michigan. Given that the Michigan office of Burger King (P) was solely charged with dealing with Rudzewicz (D), he had no reasonable expectation of being sued elsewhere.

▶ ANALYSIS

The basis of a finding of personal jurisdiction rests on the question whether compelling the defendant to defend himself in the forum state comports with due process. The Court in this case appears to infer a type of consent to jurisdiction based on the choice of law provision. As personal jurisdiction may be consented to, the Court has opened the door to a wider scope of liability.

Quicknotes

DUE PROCESS The constitutional mandate requiring the courts to protect and enforce individuals' rights and liberties consistent with prevailing principles of fairness and justice and prohibiting the federal and state governments from such activities that deprive its citizens of a life, liberty or property interest.

FORUM STATE The state in which a court, or other location in which a legal remedy may be sought, is located.

PERSONAL JURISDICTION The court's authority over a person or parties to a lawsuit.

PURPOSEFUL AVAILMENT An element in determining whether a defendant had the required minimum contacts in a forum necessary in order for a court to exercise jurisdiction over the party, whereby the court determines whether the defendant intentionally conducted activities in the forum and thus knows, or could reasonably expect, that such conduct could give rise to litigation in that forum.

Helicopteros Nacionales de Colombia, S.A. v. Hall

Colombian corporation (D) v. Employee's heir (P)

466 U.S. 408 (1984).

NATURE OF CASE: Appeal from award of damages for wrongful death.

FACT SUMMARY: Helicopteros Nacionales de Colombia, S.A. (Helicol) (D) contended the Texas courts lacked personal jurisdiction over it due to a lack of minimum contacts with the state.

🏛 RULE OF LAW
A defendant's contacts with the forum state must constitute continuous and systematic general business contacts in order for the forum state to exercise personal jurisdiction over it.

FACTS: Helicopteros Nacionales de Colombia, S.A. (Helicol) (D), a Colombian corporation with a principal place of business in Bogota, owned a helicopter which crashed in Peru, killing several U.S. citizens. The citizens were employees of a joint venture headquartered in Texas. Hall (P) and other heirs of the employees sued for wrongful death in Texas state court. Helicol (D) moved to dismiss, contending the Texas court lacked personal jurisdiction over it. The trial court denied the motion, and the jury found against Helicol (D). The court of appeals reversed, holding that Helicol's (D) contacts with Texas, essentially the attendance by a Helicol (D) executive at one meeting in Houston and the purchasing of helicopters and parts in Ft. Worth, were insufficient to constitute the requisite minimum contacts. The Texas Supreme Court reversed, and Helicol (D) appealed.

ISSUE: Does a defendant's contacts with the forum state have to constitute continuous and systematic general business contacts to allow for personal jurisdiction?

HOLDING AND DECISION: (Blackmun, J.) Yes. A defendant's contacts with the forum state must constitute continuous and systematic general business contacts in order for the forum state to exercise personal jurisdiction. It has long been held that purchases and occasional trips to the forum will not, standing alone, establish the requisite minimum contacts. Therefore, because no further showing was made concerning the contacts, the Texas courts lacked personal jurisdiction. Reversed.

DISSENT: (Brennan, J.) The relationship between the contacts and the cause of action in this case establishes sufficient contacts to support a finding of personal jurisdiction.

▌ ANALYSIS

The dissent points out that while the contacts involved may not support general personal jurisdiction, if the particular claim arises out of such contacts, jurisdiction over such claim may exist. The purchases in Ft. Worth were arguably related to the wrongful death claim as they were purchases of helicopter parts, some of which may have been used in the ill-fated helicopter.

Quicknotes

DUE PROCESS The constitutional mandate requiring the courts to protect and enforce individuals' rights and liberties consistent with prevailing principles of fairness and justice and prohibiting the federal and state governments from such activities that deprive its citizens of a life, liberty or property interest.

MINIMUM CONTACTS The minimum degree of contact necessary in order to sustain a cause of action within a particular forum, consistent with the requirements of due process.

PERSONAL JURISDICTION The court's authority over a person or parties to a lawsuit.

WRONGFUL DEATH An action brought by the beneficiaries of a deceased person, claiming that the deceased's death was the result of wrongful conduct by the defendant.

Shaffer v. Heitner

Corporation (D) v. Shareholder (P)

433 U.S. 186 (1977).

NATURE OF CASE: Appeal from a finding of state jurisdiction.

FACT SUMMARY: Heitner (P) brought a derivative suit against Greyhound (D) directors for antitrust losses it had sustained in Oregon. The suit was brought in Delaware, Greyhound's (D) state of incorporation.

RULE OF LAW
Jurisdiction cannot be founded on property within a state unless there are sufficient contacts within the meaning of the test developed in *International Shoe*.

FACTS: Heitner (P) owned one share of Greyhound (D) stock. Greyhound (D) had been subjected to a large antitrust judgment in Oregon. Heitner (P), a nonresident of Delaware, brought a derivative suit in Delaware, the state of Greyhound's (D) incorporation. Jurisdiction was based on sequestration of Greyhound (D) stock, which was deemed to be located within the state of incorporation. The Delaware sequestration statute allowed property within the state to be seized ex parte to compel the owner to submit to the in personam jurisdiction of the court. None of the stock was actually in Delaware, but a freeze order was placed on the corporate books. Greyhound (D) made a special appearance to challenge the court's jurisdiction to hear the matter. Greyhound (D) argued that the sequestration statute was unconstitutional under the line of cases beginning with *Sniadach*, 395 U.S. 337 (1969). Greyhound (D) also argued that there were insufficient contacts with Delaware to justify an exercise of jurisdiction. The Delaware courts found that the sequestration statute was valid since it was not a per se seizure of the property and was merely invoked to compel out-of-state residents to defend actions within the state. Little or no consideration was given to the "contact" argument based on a finding that the presence of the stock within the state conferred quasi in rem jurisdiction.

ISSUE: May a state assume jurisdiction over an issue merely because defendant's property happens to be within the state?

HOLDING AND DECISION: (Marshall, J.) No. Mere presence of property within a state is insufficient to confer jurisdiction on a court absent independent contacts within the meaning of International Shoe which would make acceptance constitutional. It is expressly disapproved of that the line of cases represented by *Harris v. Balk* permits jurisdiction merely because the property happens to be within the state. If sufficient contacts do not exist to assume jurisdiction absent the presence of property within the state, it cannot be invoked on the basis of property within the court's jurisdiction. This decision is based on the fundamental concepts of justice and fair play required

under the due process and equal protection clauses of the Fourteenth Amendment. Here, the stock is not the subject of the controversy. There is no claim to ownership of it or injury caused by it. The defendants do not reside in Delaware or have any contacts there. The injury occurred in Oregon. No activities complained of were done within the forum. Finally, Heitner (P) is not even a Delaware resident. Jurisdiction was improperly granted. Reversed.

CONCURRENCE: (Powell, J.) Disagreement is with cases involving property permanently within the state, e.g., real property. Such property should confer jurisdiction.

CONCURRENCE: (Stevens, J.) Concurrence is in the result since purchase of stock in the marketplace should not confer in rem jurisdiction in the state of incorporation. Concurrence is also with Mr. Justice Powell's statements.

CONCURRENCE AND DISSENT: (Brennan, J.) Concurrence is with the use of a minimum contacts test, but dissent as to the result in this case. The Delaware sequestration statute's sole purpose is to force in personam jurisdiction through a quasi in rem seizure. The opinion is purely advisory in that if the court finds the statute invalid, the rest of the opinion is not required. Delaware never argued that it was attempting to obtain in rem jurisdiction. Further, it is held that a derivative suit may be brought in the state of incorporation. Greyhound's (D) choice of incorporation in Delaware is a prima facie showing of submission to its jurisdiction.

ANALYSIS

While the corporation could be sued in its state of incorporation under the dissents' theory, the suit is against the directors and neither the site of the wrong nor the residence of a defendant is in Delaware. The decision will have a major impact only in cases such as herein where the state really has no reason to want to adjudicate the issue. Of course real property would still be treated as an exception.

━━■

Quicknotes

ATTACHMENT The seizing of the property of one party in anticipation of, or in order to satisfy, a favorable judgment obtained by another party.

IN REM JURISDICTION A court's authority over an object so that its judgment is binding in respect to the rights and interests of all parties in that object.

QUASI IN REM A court's authority over the defendant's property within a specified geographical area.

━━■

Burnham v. Superior Court of California

New Jersey citizen (D) v. State court (P)

495 U.S. 604 (1990).

NATURE OF CASE: Review of denial of mandamus arising out of a motion to quash for lack of jurisdiction in an action for dissolution.

FACT SUMMARY: Burnham (D) contended that service of process upon him while he was present in the forum state was invalid because he lacked minimum contacts therewith.

🏛 RULE OF LAW
A state need not have minimum contacts with a defendant to exercise jurisdiction over him if he is served with process while physically present therein.

FACTS: Dennis (D) and Francie (P) Burnham lived in New Jersey. The couple separated, and Francie (P) moved to California. While in California on business, Dennis (D) stopped by to visit his daughter. He was then served with dissolution papers. He moved to quash service, contending that he lacked minimum contacts with California. The motion was denied. Dennis (D) petitioned for mandamus, which the court of appeal denied. The California Supreme Court denied certiorari, but the U.S. Supreme Court granted review.

ISSUE: Must a state have minimum contacts with a defendant to exercise jurisdiction over him if he is served with process while physically present therein?

HOLDING AND DECISION: (Scalia, J.) No. A state need not have minimum contacts with a defendant to exercise jurisdiction over him if he is served with process while physically present therein. It has long been an assumption of Anglo-American law, and certainly was so at the time the Fourteenth Amendment was adopted, that a state may fully exercise its jurisdiction over a person in that state. Authority on this point is scarce, but this appears to be because it has always been assumed to be true and therefore has not been much litigated. This Court has held that "minimum contacts" must exist for jurisdiction to be exercised over an absent defendant, but the operative word is absent. Minimum contacts have always been a substitute for physical presence and are completely irrelevant when a defendant can be found in a jurisdiction. Here, Dennis (D) was served while in California, so no minimum contacts analysis was necessary. Affirmed.

CONCURRENCE: (White, J.) Some cases may exist where physical presence alone cannot confer jurisdiction, but this is not.

CONCURRENCE: (Brennan, J.) The majority opinion gives undue importance to historic pedigree in terms of constitutionality. Pedigree alone does not confer constitutionality. The in-state service rule comports with due process, and inquiry into its historical roots, although relevant, is not dispositive.

CONCURRENCE: (Stevens, J.) The decision here was very easy to make, and the Court has overanalyzed the issue.

▶ ANALYSIS

No majority opinion was issued here. Unlike some plurality-opinion cases, however, there is no question about the effect of the decision. All nine of the justices would appear to concur that the in-state service rule would be valid in all or nearly all cases.

Quicknotes

CERTIORARI A discretionary writ issued by a superior court to an inferior court in order to review the lower court's decisions; the Supreme Court's writ ordering such review.

DISSOLUTION Annulment or termination of a formal or legal bond, tie or contract.

DUE PROCESS The constitutional mandate requiring the courts to protect and enforce individuals' rights and liberties consistent with prevailing principles of fairness and justice and prohibiting the federal and state governments from such activities that deprive its citizens of a life, liberty or property interest.

MANDAMUS A court order issued commanding a public or private entity, or an official thereof, to perform a duty required by law.

MINIMUM CONTACTS The minimum degree of contact necessary in order to sustain a cause of action within a particular forum, consistent with the requirements of due process.

Piper Aircraft v. Reyno

U.S. companies (D) v. U.S. plaintiff (P)

454 U.S. 235 (1981).

NATURE OF CASE: Appeal of judgment denying dismissal based on forum non conveniens.

FACT SUMMARY: A plane crashed in Scotland killing six people, all of whom were Scottish. A wrongful death lawsuit was filed in a U.S. court on behalf of the decedents. The makers of the plane and the propeller, both of which were companies based in the United States, were named as defendants. The trial court granted the defendants' motion to dismiss, on forum non conveniens grounds. The federal court of appeals reversed and remanded to trial.

> ## 🏛 RULE OF LAW
> (1) The possibility of an unfavorable change in law does not bar dismissal on the ground of forum non conveniens.
> (2) The presumption in favor of the plaintiff's forum choice applies with less than maximum force where the real parties in interest are foreign and private and public interests favor trial outside the United States.

FACTS: In 1976, a plane crashed in Scotland killing six people, all of whom were Scottish. The twin-engine plane was manufactured in Pennsylvania by Piper Aircraft (D), and the propellers were manufactured in Ohio by Hartzell Propeller, Inc. (D). The aircraft was registered in Great Britain and was owned and maintained by Air Navigation and Trading Co. It was operated by McDonald Aviation, Ltd., a Scottish air taxi service. The court appointed administratrix of the estates of the five passengers, Gaynell Reyno (P), filed a wrongful death lawsuit in a U.S. court on behalf of the decedents. The lawsuit named Piper (D) and Hartzell (D) as defendants, but not Air Navigation and Trading or McDonald Aviation. Reyno (P) admits that the action against Piper (D) and Hartzell (D) was filed in the United States because its laws on the issues were more favorable to her case than Scottish laws. Piper (D) and Hartzell (D) moved to dismiss on the ground of forum non conveniens, and the district court granted the motions. The Third Circuit Court of Appeals reversed and remanded to trial.

ISSUE:

(1) Does the possibility of an unfavorable change in law bar dismissal on the ground of forum non conveniens?

(2) Does the presumption in favor of the plaintiff's forum choice apply with less than maximum force where the real parties in interest are foreign and private and public interests favor trial outside the United States?

HOLDING AND DECISION: (Marshall, J.)

(1) No. The possibility of an unfavorable change in law does not bar dismissal on the ground of forum non conveniens. While the possibility of an unfavorable change in law should sometimes be a relevant consideration in a forum non conveniens inquiry, such as when the remedy provided by the alternative forum is so clearly inadequate or unsatisfactory that it is no remedy at all. But in this case, the remedies that would be provided by the Scottish courts do not fall in that category. There is no danger here that the relatives of the decedents will be deprived of any remedy or treated unfairly. In addition, if substantial weight were given to the possibility of a change in law, dismissal would rarely be proper, and the forum non conveniens doctrine would become virtually useless. Finally, if the possibility of a change in law were given substantial weight, deciding motions to dismiss on the ground of forum non conveniens would become difficult, and choice-of-law analysis would become more important, and courts would frequently be required to interpret the law of foreign jurisdictions. American courts, which are already extremely attractive to foreign plaintiffs, would become even more attractive. The flow of litigation into the United States would increase and further congest already crowded courts.

(2) Yes. The presumption in favor of the plaintiff's forum choice applies with less than maximum force where the real parties in interest are foreign and private and public interests favor trial outside the United States. Under *Gulf Oil Corp. v. Gilbert*, 330 U.S. 501 (1947), dismissal will be appropriate where trial in the plaintiff's chosen forum imposes a heavy burden on the defendant or the court, and where the plaintiff is unable to offer any specific reasons of convenience supporting his choice. Having determined that the plaintiff's choice of forum deserved less deference because the real parties in interest are foreign, the district court properly turned to balancing the private interests of the plaintiffs and defendants, as well as consideration of the public interests. When the forum has been chosen, it is reasonable to assume that this choice is convenient, but when the plaintiff is foreign, this assumption is much less reasonable. Because the central purpose of any forum non conveniens inquiry is to ensure that the trial is convenient, a foreign plaintiff's choice deserves less deference. In addition, the district court reasonably considered the private and public interests would be best served if the trial were held in Scotland. The district court correctly concluded that

Continued on next page.

the problems posed by the inability to implead potential third-party defendants supported holding the trial in Scotland. In addition, the factors relating to the public interest were also reasonable. Scotland has a very strong interest in this litigation. Reversed.

DISSENT: (Stevens, J.) Whereas a motion to dismiss on forum non conveniens grounds should not be denied simply because the alternate forum is less favorable to recovery, the case should be remanded to determine whether the district court correctly decided that Pennsylvania was not a convenient forum.

▶ *ANALYSIS*

In footnote 6 of the opinion, the court lists the private and public interests that are balanced in a *Gilbert* inquiry, but the court does not state how factors are balanced to reach a conclusion.

■═■

Quicknotes

FORUM NON CONVENIENS An equitable doctrine permitting a court to refrain from hearing and determining a case when the matter may be more properly and fairly heard in another forum.

■═■

CHAPTER 5

Recognition of Judgments

Quick Reference Rules of Law

Fauntleroy v. Lum

[Parties not identified.]

210 U.S. 230 (1908).

NATURE OF CASE: Suit to enforce contract indebtedness.

FACT SUMMARY: Lum (P) brought suit in Mississippi to enforce a Missouri judgment in his favor arising out of a contract executed and performed in Mississippi but not enforceable there due to illegality.

🏛 RULE OF LAW
A judgment rendered by a court of competent jurisdiction in one state is entitled to full faith and credit in another state notwithstanding any errors of law in the judgment or the fact that the underlying cause of action is prohibited in the second state.

FACTS: Lum's (P) predecessor in interest entered into a commodities futures contract with Fauntleroy (D) in Mississippi. Such contracts were in violation of both civil and criminal statutes of Mississippi. An arbitration proceeding resulted in an award to Lum (P) under the contract. Lum (P) then sued in Missouri to enforce the award and judgment was granted in his favor. He then brought suit in Mississippi to enforce the Missouri judgment, but the Mississippi court refused enforcement because to do so would be in violation of express public policy.

ISSUE: Must the courts of one state give full faith and credit enforcement to the judgment of another state based on an agreement which violates the public policy of the state asked to enforce the judgment?

HOLDING AND DECISION: (Holmes, J.) Yes. The judgment of a state court should have the same credit, validity, and effect in every other court in the United States which it had in the state where it was pronounced, and whatever pleas would be good to a suit thereon in such state, and no others, could be pleaded in any other court of the United States. If the judgment of the Missouri court was based on a mistake of Mississippi law, then that judgment could have been appealed in Missouri. Since it was not, it is as enforceable in Mississippi as it would be in Missouri. Reversed.

DISSENT: (White, J.) Full faith and credit is a constitutional mandate of the common law concept of comity and was not intended to create new powers. The doctrine of comity never imposed an obligation on one jurisdiction to enforce a foreign judgment that violated its own public policy. The majority's decision obliterates the sovereignty of each state to legislate in its own perceived interests.

▶ ANALYSIS

The merits of a foreign judgment can never be examined when enforcement is sought in the forum state. The only legitimate challenge can be to the jurisdiction, personal or subject matter, of the foreign court to render the judgment. The majority opinion in this case has been affirmed as late as 1949 by the Supreme Court.

■■■

Quicknotes

ARBITRATION An agreement to have a dispute heard and decided by a neutral third party, rather than through legal proceedings.

COMITY A rule pursuant to which courts in one state give deference to the statutes and judicial decisions of another.

FULL FAITH AND CREDIT CLAUSE State judicial proceedings shall have such faith and credit given them in every court in the United States as they would in their own state.

MEDIA CONCLUDENDI The elements upon which a legal determination is based.

PUBLIC POLICY Policy administered by the state with respect to the health, safety and morals of its people in accordance with common notions of fairness and decency.

■■■

Yarborough v. Yarborough

Father (D) v. Daughter (P)

290 U.S. 202 (1933).

NATURE OF CASE: Child support, education, and maintenance award appealed by father (D) from South Carolina Supreme Court on argument that prior Georgia decision is entitled to full faith and credit and res judicata.

FACT SUMMARY: Father (D), a Georgia resident, contested the support award made by the South Carolina court to his daughter (P), a domiciliary of South Carolina, on the ground that a Georgia judgment, pursuant to his divorce, was satisfied and has freed him of all further obligations to the child (P).

> ## 🏛 RULE OF LAW
> A state must give full faith and credit to a final judgment of another state, notwithstanding that the prior judgment has a bearing on the internal affairs of the state not foreseen at the time of the original judgment.

FACTS: The plaintiff father was sued by his daughter (P) through her grandfather as guardian ad litem in South Carolina. Sadie (P), the daughter, asked for support for education and maintenance, claiming that without such support she would be dependent upon charity. Jurisdiction was obtained over the father (D) and over some of his property in South Carolina. The plaintiff father contended that a prior Georgia judgment in a divorce suit with the child's (P) mother had determined his entire obligation to his daughter (P), and this obligation having been satisfied was res judicata and entitled to full faith and credit. Sadie (P) argued that the Georgia judgment should not be res judicata because

(1) she was not a party to that suit,
(2) she was not a domiciliary of Georgia at the time of the judgment,
(3) she was now a domiciliary of South Carolina which had its own laws of support,
(4) she had a need now which her father (D) could afford to and should be obligated to meet and, finally,
(5) the Georgia court had not intended to bar other interested states from acting in the future but had only litigated the question concerning its own interests, under its own laws. The trial court found for Sadie, the child (P), and ordered plaintiff father's property in South Carolina to be held as security for performance of its support order. The South Carolina Supreme Court upheld the trial court's award of $50 monthly to be paid to the grandfather as trustee for Sadie's (P) education and support plus attorney fees. The U.S. Supreme Court reversed on appeal and held for the father (D).

ISSUE: Is a court required to give full faith and credit to a judgment of a sister state's court where that judgment affects vital interests of that second state not in existence at the time of the judgment?

HOLDING AND DECISION: (Brandeis, J.) Yes. Full faith and credit must be given to the Georgia judgment, and that judgment is res judicata between the parties, notwithstanding the present interest of South Carolina in the welfare of its domiciliary, the child (P), whose rights were determined by that prior judgment. The court found that Sadie (P), although not a party to the Georgia divorce, was nevertheless bound by the decree under Georgia law concerning her right to support from her father (D). Further, the court found that Sadie's (P) domiciliary was Georgia at the time, according to the rule that a minor takes the domicile of her father, which was Georgia until the divorce decree was final, regardless of the fact that she was not living there at the time. Reversed.

DISSENT: (Stone, J.) The Georgia judgment is final insofar as Georgia's interest in the case is concerned, but that judgment should not be allowed to dictate events in the future beyond Georgia boundaries. The internal interests of South Carolina entitle it to make the new judgment for the welfare of its domiciliary and the Full Faith and Credit Clause does not demand that South Carolina uphold the Georgia judgment in this case as a bar to its own action. The Supreme Court should be able to limit the operation of the Full Faith and Credit Clause to allow South Carolina to take into account the present needs of the child which might justify a further award against the father, who is still domiciled in Georgia. To give the Georgia judgment the effect given it by the majority is to expand it beyond the reasonable demands of the constitutional requirement of full faith and credit.

▶ ANALYSIS

The *Yarborough* case left open the question of whether the result would have been the same if the father (D) had also changed his domicile. However, in *Elkind v. Byck*, 68 Cal. 2d 453, 67 Cal. Rptr. 404, 439 P.2d 316 (1968), the court held that the *Yarborough* decision would not control where the father had changed his home state and moved to California since the earlier decree. Thus, Justice Stone's dissent, which sought to limit the effect of the Full Faith and Credit Clause where a judgment rendered by one state later impinged on the internal affairs of another, was echoed in later decisions. Courts have found that an earlier judgment

Continued on next page.

was not meant to foreclose another state with a compelling interest from acting upon changes in circumstances at a future date, particularly in the area of support where the parties to the original judgment have changed domicile.

■══■

Quicknotes

FULL FAITH AND CREDIT ACT State judicial proceedings shall have such faith and credit given them in every court in the United States as they would in their own state.

■══■

Thomas v. Washington Gas Light Co.

Disabled employee (P) v. Employer (D)

448 U.S. 261 (1980).

NATURE OF CASE: Appeal from denial of award for workmen's compensation.

FACT SUMMARY: Thomas (P) contended that the obligation of the District of Columbia to give full faith and credit to an award under the Virginia Workmen's Compensation Act did not bar a supplemental award under a similar act.

> **🏛 RULE OF LAW**
> The Full Faith and Credit Clause should not be construed to preclude successive workmen's compensation awards.

FACTS: Thomas (P) received an award of disability benefits under the Virginia Workmen's Compensation Act in 1971, for injuries suffered in Virginia. In 1974, Thomas (P), a resident of the District of Columbia, notified the Department of Labor of his intention to seek compensation under the District of Columbia Act. Washington (D) opposed the request, arguing that the obligation of the District of Columbia to give full faith and credit to the Virginia award barred a supplemental award under the District's Workmen's Compensation Act. The Court of Appeals for the Fourth Circuit, in reversing the decision of the district court, held that a second and separate proceeding in another jurisdiction upon the same injury, after a prior recovery in another state was precluded by the Full Faith and Credit Clause. Thomas (P) then brought this appeal.

ISSUE: Should the Full Faith and Credit Clause be construed to preclude successive workmen's compensation awards?

HOLDING AND DECISION: (Stevens, J.) No. The Full Faith and Credit Clause should not be construed to preclude successive workmen's compensation awards. Typically, a workmen's compensation tribunal may apply only its own state's law. The Virginia Commission could and did establish the full measure of Thomas's (P) rights under Virginia law, but it could not purport to determine his rights under the law of the District of Columbia. A state has no legitimate interest within the context of our federal system in preventing another state from granting a supplemental compensation award when that second state would have had the power to apply its workmen's compensation law in the first instance. Reversed.

CONCURRENCE: (White, J.) There is no reason why a judgment should not be entitled to full res judicata effect under the Full Faith and Credit Clause merely because the rendering tribunal was obligated to apply the law of the forum.

DISSENT: (Rehnquist, J.) Unless the District of Columbia has an interest in forcing its residents to accept its law regardless of their wishes, the Virginia Commission's inability to look to District of Columbia law did not impinge upon the District of Columbia's jurisdictional interests.

▶ ANALYSIS

The majority in this case distinguished and perhaps overruled the holding in *Industrial Commission of Wisconsin v. McCartin*, 330 U.S. 622 (1947), that authorized a state, by drafting or construing its legislation in "unmistakable language," directly to determine the extraterritorial effect of its workmen's compensation awards.

◼▬◼

Quicknotes

FULL FAITH AND CREDIT ACT State judicial proceedings shall have such faith and credit given them in every court in the United States as they would in their own state.

RES JUDICATA The rule of law that a final judgment by a court precludes subsequent litigation between the parties regarding the same cause of action.

◼▬◼

Durfee v. Duke

Property owner (D) v. Adjacent owner (P)

375 U.S. 106 (1963).

NATURE OF CASE: Appeal from an action to determine ownership to land.

FACT SUMMARY: After Durfee (D) won a Nebraska case determining that certain land was in fact in Nebraska and belonged to him, Duke (P) began a new action in Missouri, where the U.S. Court of Appeals held the Nebraska action not to be res judicata on the issues.

RULE OF LAW
A judgment is entitled to full faith and credit, even as to questions of jurisdiction, when the questions have been fully and fairly litigated and decided in the court which rendered the original judgment.

FACTS: Durfee (D) brought an action in Nebraska to quiet title to certain bottom land along the Missouri River. The river's main channel is the boundary between Nebraska and Missouri. Nebraska had jurisdiction over the subject matter only if the land was, in fact, in Nebraska. In full litigation of the issues, the Nebraska court found that it had jurisdiction. It then determined that Durfee (D) owned the land. The Nebraska Supreme Court affirmed and Duke (P) did not appeal further. Two months later, Duke (P) brought suit in Missouri to quiet title to the same land. By diversity of citizenship, the action was removed to federal district court which decided that while the land appeared to be in Missouri, the Nebraska ruling was res judicata on the issues and binding. The court of appeals reversed, and Durfee (D) appealed.

ISSUE: Is a judgment entitled to full faith and credit, even as to questions of jurisdiction, when the second court's inquiry discloses that those questions have been fully and fairly litigated and finally decided in the court which rendered the original judgment?

HOLDING AND DECISION: (Stewart, J.) Yes. A judgment is entitled to full faith and credit, even as to questions of jurisdiction, when the second court's inquiry discloses that those questions have been fully and fairly litigated and finally decided in the court which rendered the original judgment. Public policy requires that litigation come to an end at some time. The litigants must reach a point where they will be bound by the ruling. The general rule is no different when the issue is one of jurisdiction. When a case is fully heard and there has been no fraud, the parties are bound by the court to which they submitted their dispute. While certain exceptions such as federal preemption or sovereign immunity exist, none apply here. All issues were fully litigated in the Nebraska courts including the issue of jurisdiction. Full faith and credit must be given the Nebraska ruling. Reversed.

CONCURRENCE: (Black, J.) The court is not deciding the outcome if the states were to agree the land was in Missouri.

ANALYSIS

The older view allowed a second court to examine the jurisdictional basis upon which the first court ruled. Jurisdiction is no longer a "magic word," but is approached as any other issue. Restatement of Conflicts, Second, § 97, suggests a balancing test to determine whether subject matter jurisdiction should be allowed to be collaterally attacked. Such balancing depends on policy considerations including whether the determination is based on questions of fact or law, and whether the question was actually litigated.

Quicknotes

COLLATERAL ATTACK A proceeding initiated in order to challenge the integrity of a previous judgment.

DOMICILE A person's permanent home or principal establishment to which he has an intention of returning when he is absent therefrom.

PUBLIC POLICY Policy administered by the state with respect to the health, safety and morals of its people in accordance with common notions of fairness and decency.

QUIET TITLE Equitable action to resolve conflicting claims to an interest in real property.

RES JUDICATA The rule of law that a final judgment by a court precludes subsequent litigation between the parties regarding the same cause of action.

SOVEREIGN IMMUNITY Immunity of government from suit without its consent.

SUBJECT MATTER JURISDICTION The authority of the court to hear and decide actions involving a particular type of issue or subject.

Clarke v. Clarke

Father (P) v. Daughter (D)

178 U.S. 186 (1900).

NATURE OF CASE: Administrator's petition seeking instructions.

FACT SUMMARY: Connecticut refused to recognize a prior South Carolina decision construing Mrs. Clarke's will as working an equitable conversion of the property she had owned in Connecticut into personalty to pass as such under the will.

🏛 RULE OF LAW
The courts of the state where a decedent's land is situated are not bound to recognize another jurisdiction's decision as to how her will affects the status of such land.

FACTS: A South Carolina resident, Mrs. Clarke died leaving a will that directed an equal division of her real and personal property between her husband, Mr. Clarke (P), and their two daughters. One daughter, Julia, died within a short time thereafter. Mr. Clarke (P) served as administrator of his wife's estate and as administrator of his deceased daughter. He sued in South Carolina to obtain a construction of his wife's will, his remaining daughter Nancy (D) being represented by a guardian ad litem. That court held the will worked an equitable conversion of the wife's real property, including that which was located in Connecticut, so that it would be distributed as personalty. When Mr. Clarke (P) brought a Connecticut action seeking instructions, the court there refused to recognize the South Carolina decision on how the will affected the status of the Connecticut property and ruled that the Connecticut land was to pass as real property according to Connecticut law. Mr. Clarke (P) appealed, claiming that the South Carolina decree was entitled to full faith and credit.

ISSUE: Must the courts in the state where a decedent's land is located honor another jurisdiction's decision as to how her will affects the status of such land?

HOLDING AND DECISION: (White, J.) No. The courts in the state where a decedent's land is located are not required to honor another jurisdiction's decision as to how her will affects the status of such land. The reason is that such land is not a subject matter directly amenable to the jurisdiction of the courts of non-situs states. Thus, there was no requirement that the South Carolina decision on the issue of how the will affected the Connecticut land be given full faith and credit. Affirmed.

▶ ANALYSIS

Baxter criticizes the traditional notion that the situs state always has exclusive jurisdiction over land. He comments:

"The historical reason for the traditional situs reference—legal acquiescence in the de facto power of the situs state to effectuate its policies—has no relevance to our federal system." Choice of Law and the Federal System, 16 Stan. L. Rev. 1, 15-17 (1963).

Quicknotes

DOMICILE A person's permanent home or principal establishment to which he has an intention of returning when he is absent therefrom.

EQUITABLE CONVERSION Doctrine pursuant to which once property is sold pursuant to a land sale contract, equitable title passes to the buyer and legal title remains in the seller as security until the remainder of the purchase price is tendered.

FULL FAITH AND CREDIT Doctrine that a judgment by a court of one state shall be given the same effect in another state.

Fall v. Eastin

Wife (P) v. Husband's grantee (D)

215 U.S. 1 (1909).

NATURE OF CASE: Suit to quiet title to realty.

FACT SUMMARY: As part of a divorce settlement decree rendered in Washington, Mrs. Fall (P) received title to certain Nebraska real estate by way of a commissioner's deed. She then sought to quiet title in Nebraska against a subsequent grantee—Eastin (D)—of the property.

RULE OF LAW
The courts of one state cannot directly affect title to real property in another state by a decree and commissioner's deed in equity, and such decree and deed are not entitled to full faith and credit outside the state where rendered.

FACTS: In connection with a divorce property settlement in the state of Washington, Mrs. Fall (P) was awarded certain real property owned by her husband in Washington. When he failed to obey a valid in personam order to convey title to her, the Washington court, through an equity commissioner, executed a deed in her favor. The husband then conveyed the land to Eastin (D) and Mrs. Fall (P) brought a quiet title action in Nebraska based on the Washington decree and deed. The husband was not a party to the Nebraska suit. The Nebraska court refused full faith and credit recognition of the commissioner's deed or the decree supporting it.

ISSUE: May the courts of one state directly affect title to real estate located in another state by way of an in rem decree or commissioner's deed?

HOLDING AND DECISION: (McKenna, J.) No. A court of equity, having valid jurisdiction over the person, may order the owner of real property located elsewhere to convey that property by proper deed. This order can be enforced through contempt citation. By this method, the court can indirectly affect title to realty located outside the state. But the court cannot affect such property directly by an in rem order or commissioner's deed. The Washington commissioner's deed was not entitled to full faith and credit recognition in Nebraska, since Washington did not have valid jurisdiction over the property. Since the husband was not a party to the *Nebraska* action, the decree was not enforceable against him there. Affirmed.

CONCURRENCE: (Holmes, J.) The Nebraska decision was based on that court's view that the decree was an in rem order issued by a court without valid jurisdiction over the property. If the Washington decree were pursued as an in personam order against the husband, it would be entitled to full faith and credit in Nebraska if valid jurisdiction over the husband could be had. But, viewed in the light of an in rem order, the Nebraska court's decision is not reviewable by this court.

ANALYSIS

The decision in this case has been the subject for much debate since its rendition. The principle laid down stands as valid law to the present time, however. The apparent inconsistency of prohibiting direct action as against out-of-state real property while sanctioning coerced deeds also remains.

Quicknotes

DEED A signed writing transferring title to real property from one person to another.

FULL FAITH AND CREDIT Doctrine that a judgment by a court of one state shall be given the same effect in another state.

IN PERSONAM An action against a person seeking to impose personal liability.

IN REM An action against property.

QUIET TITLE Equitable action to resolve conflicting claims to an interest in real property.

Worthley v. Worthley

Wife (P) v. Former husband (D)

Cal. Sup. Ct., 44 Cal. 2d 465, 283 P.2d 19 (1955).

NATURE OF CASE: Suit to enforce judgment for alimony arrearages.

FACT SUMMARY: Mrs. Worthley (P) sought to recover alimony arrearages in California based on a modifiable New Jersey decree and to establish the New Jersey decree as a California decree as to future installments.

🏛 RULE OF LAW
A state may validly enforce payment of alimony arrearages and future installments based on a sister state's modifiable decree if both parties are before the court and the issue of modification can be litigated as to both parties.

FACTS: Mrs. Worthley (P) received a judgment for alimony in New Jersey which was modifiable both retroactively and prospectively. She sought to enforce a claim for arrearages in California and to have the California court establish the decree as a California judgment as to future installments. The trial court entered judgment for Mr. Worthley (D).

ISSUE: May a state enforce a modifiable decree for alimony rendered elsewhere when both parties are before the present court and the issue of modification can be litigated?

HOLDING AND DECISION: (Traynor, J.) Yes. While the courts of one state are not bound to enforce the modifiable decree of another state, they may choose to do so. California is entitled to give such credit to the previous decree as it would receive in the state where it was rendered. California may litigate the issue of modification, either retroactive or prospective, in the same manner as the rendering state so long as both parties are properly before the court. Any judgment for arrearages after consideration of modification will be final and enforceable anywhere. A judgment for future installments will be a California judgment enforceable, except for potential modifications, here or anywhere. Reversed.

DISSENT: (Spence, J.) As long as the New Jersey judgment is not final due to its modifiability, California is bound not to enforce it. This decree is modifiable by any state at any time according to the majority, a view that will result in unacceptable confusion.

▶ ANALYSIS

The view of the majority is being adopted by an increasing number of jurisdictions. Once the second state has imposed its own decree, it may enforce that decree by appropriate measures, including sequestration and contempt. Some courts have enforced sister state modifiable decrees on the basis that to deny enforcement would create sanctuaries for those seeking to avoid their obligations.

Quicknotes

FINAL JUDGMENT A decision by the court settling a dispute between the parties on its merits and which is appealable to a higher court.

FULL FAITH AND CREDIT Doctrine that a judgment by a court of one state shall be given the same effect in another state.

SEQUESTRATION ORDER A court order requiring the attachment of property or funds, pending a final disposition in the action.

Baker v. General Motors Corporation

Decedent's estate (P) v. Auto manufacturer (D)

522 U.S. 222 (1998).

NATURE OF CASE: Review of reversal of judgment enforcing an injunction forbidding a witness from appearing in certain court proceedings.

FACT SUMMARY: After an injunction had been issued in one state court prohibiting a former employee from testifying as a witness, Baker (P) subpoenaed the same former employee to appear as a witness in another state in litigation against the same employer, General Motors Corporation (D).

RULE OF LAW

Orders commanding action or inaction may be denied enforcement in a sister state when they purport to accomplish an official act within the exclusive province of that other state or interfere with litigation over which the ordering state has no authority.

FACTS: In settlement of claims arising from the discharge of Elwell, a former employee of General Motors Corporation (D), a state court in Michigan issued a permanent injunction barring Elwell from testifying, without the prior written consent of GM (D), as a witness of any kind in any litigation involving GM (D). GM (D) separately agreed, however, that if Elwell were ordered to testify by a court, such testimony would not be actionable. The Bakers (P) sued GM (D) in Missouri and subpoenaed Elwell to appear as a witness in their suit. The federal district court in Missouri allowed the Bakers (P) to depose Elwell and call him as a witness at trial. Relying on the Full Faith and Credit Clause, the Eighth Circuit reversed, ruling that the testimony should not have been admitted. The Supreme Court granted review.

ISSUE: May orders commanding action or inaction be denied enforcement in a sister state when they purport to accomplish an official act within the exclusive province of that other state or interfere with litigation over which the ordering state has no authority?

HOLDING AND DECISION: (Ginsburg, J.) Yes. Orders commanding action or inaction may be denied enforcement in a sister state when they purport to accomplish an official act within the exclusive province of that other state or interfere with litigation over which the ordering state has no authority. In this case, the Michigan decree ordering the injunction cannot determine evidentiary issues in a lawsuit brought by parties who were not subject to the jurisdiction of the Michigan court. The Full Faith and Credit Clause mandates recognition only of dispositions that Michigan has the authority to order. A Michigan decree cannot command obedience elsewhere

on a matter the Michigan court lacks authority to resolve. Reversed.

CONCURRENCE: (Scalia, J.) It has been established that the judgment of a state court cannot be enforced out of state by an execution issued within it.

CONCURRENCE: (Kennedy, J.) The case is controlled by well-settled full faith and credit principles which render the majority's extended analysis unnecessary. Courts need give a prior judgment no more force or effect than the issuing state gives it. Since the Bakers (P) were not parties to the Michigan proceedings and had no opportunity to litigate any of the issues presented, it appears that Michigan law would not treat them as bound by the judgment.

ANALYSIS

The Court relied on precedent in reaching its decision. Earlier cases considered the transfer of title to land in another state to be an "official act within the exclusive province" of the situs state. The Court, however, made the point that there is no "roving 'public policy' exception" to judgment recognition under the Full Faith and Credit Clause.

Quicknotes

EXPERT WITNESS A witness providing testimony at trial who is specially qualified regarding the particular subject matter involved.

FULL FAITH AND CREDIT Doctrine that a judgment by a court of one state shall be given the same effect in another state.

INJUNCTION A court order requiring a person to do or prohibiting that person from doing a specific act.

Allen v. McCurry

Accused (P) v. Police (D)

449 U.S. 90 (1980).

NATURE OF CASE: Federal suit for damages for violation of constitutional rights.

FACT SUMMARY: After the issue of illegal search and seizure had been fully adjudicated in his state criminal trial, McCurry (P) brought a federal suit seeking damages for the alleged violation of his constitutional rights arising from the alleged illegal search and seizure.

RULE OF LAW
The rules of collateral estoppel apply to prevent one from relitigating in a federal suit for violation of constitutional rights those issues he had a "full and fair" opportunity to litigate in a prior state criminal trial against him.

FACTS: During the trial in which he was convicted of heroin and assault offenses, McCurry (P) questioned the constitutionality of the search and seizure that had occurred. The court denied his suppression motion in part, and he was convicted. He was not able to seek a federal writ of habeas corpus because he did not assert that the state courts had denied him a "full and fair" opportunity to litigate his search and seizure claim. Nonetheless, he sought federal court redress for the alleged constitutional violation by bringing a damage suit under 42 U.S.C. 1983 against the officers, including Allen (D), who had conducted the search. The district court held collateral estoppel precluded relitigation of the issue. The court of appeals reversed, concluding that the only route to a federal forum McCurry (P) had for his constitutional claim was his 1983 suit.

ISSUE: Can one relitigate in a federal suit issues decided against him in a state criminal proceeding in which he had a "full and fair" opportunity to litigate them?

HOLDING AND DECISION: (Stewart, J.) No. Section 1983 presents no categorical bar to the application of collateral estoppel concepts, which would indeed prevent one from relitigating in a federal suit alleging a violation of constitutional rights those issues decided against him in a state criminal proceeding in which he was given a "full and fair" opportunity to litigate them. Nothing guarantees that every person asserting a federal right is entitled to one unencumbered opportunity to litigate that right in a federal district court. Reversed and remanded.

DISSENT: (Blackmun, J.) A criminal defendant prosecuted in state court is an involuntary litigant in that forum who cannot be forced to a choice between foregoing either a potential defense there or a federal forum later.

ANALYSIS

The question of whether or not a deliberate or inadvertent failure to raise the search and seizure issue in the state criminal proceedings would permit it to be thereafter raised in a § 1983 suit was not addressed. The implication in Restatement Second, Judgments § 133 (Tent. Draft 7, 1980) is that it could be so raised in a subsequent federal suit.

Quicknotes

COLLATERAL ESTOPPEL A doctrine whereby issues litigated and determined in a prior proceeding are binding upon all subsequent litigation between the parties regarding that issue.

FOURTH AMENDMENT Provides that persons be secure as to their person and private belongings against unreasonable searches and seizures.

HABEAS CORPUS A proceeding in which a defendant brings a writ to compel a judicial determination of whether he is lawfully being held in custody.

Matsushita Electric Industrial Co. v. Epstein

Corporation (D) v. Shareholders (P)

516 U.S. 367 (1996).

NATURE OF CASE: Appeal from dismissal of shareholders' derivative action.

FACT SUMMARY: A state court settlement was found not to have preclusive effect because it released exclusively federal claims.

RULE OF LAW
A federal court may not withhold full faith and credit from a state-court judgment approving a class action settlement simply because the settlement releases claims within the exclusive jurisdiction of the federal courts.

FACTS: Matsushita Electric Industrial Co. (D) made a tender offer which led to Matsushita's (D) acquisition of MCA, Inc., a Delaware corporation. A class action was filed in the Delaware Court of Chancery against MCA and later, Matsushita (D), for breach of fiduciary duty in failing to maximize shareholder value. At the same time, another complaint was filed in federal court, alleging violations of Securities Exchange Commission Rules. The district court dismissed the federal action and the case was appealed to the Court of Appeals for the Ninth Circuit. Before a decision was handed down in that case, the parties to the Delaware suit negotiated a settlement. The Chancery Court certified a class for purposes of settlement and approved a notice of the proposed settlement. Epstein (P) was a member of both the state and federal plaintiff classes but failed to opt out of the settlement class or to appear at the hearing to contest the settlement or the representation of the class. On appeal in the Ninth Circuit, Matsushita (D) raised the Delaware judgment as a bar to further prosecution under the Full Faith and Credit Act. The court of appeals found that 28 U.S.C. § 1738 did not apply, and fashioned a test under which the preclusive force of a state court settlement judgment was limited to those claims that could have been extinguished by the issue preclusive effect of an adjudication of the state claims. The Supreme Court granted certiorari.

ISSUE: May a federal court withhold full faith and credit from a state-court judgment approving a class action settlement simply because the settlement releases claims within the exclusive jurisdiction of the federal courts?

HOLDING AND DECISION: (Thomas, J.) No. A federal court may not withhold full faith and credit from a state-court judgment approving a class action settlement simply because the settlement releases claims within the exclusive jurisdiction of the federal courts. A federal court must give the judgment the same effect that it would have in the courts of the state in which it was rendered. The Full Faith and Credit Act, 28 U.S.C. § 1738, is applicable to cases in which the state court judgment at issue incorporated a class action settlement releasing claims solely within the jurisdiction of the federal courts. Since Delaware has generally treated the impact of settlement judgments on subsequent state court litigation as a question of claim preclusion, Delaware would probably afford preclusive effect to the settlement in this case as well. Congress did not intend to create an exception to 28 U.S.C. § 1738 for suits alleging violations of the Exchange Act. Reversed and remanded.

ANALYSIS

The Circuit Court had decided that the Delaware court had acted outside the bounds of its own jurisdiction in approving the settlement. The Circuit Court decided that full faith and credit would not be required because the state court did not have subject matter jurisdiction. But here the U.S. Supreme Court decided that the Delaware court clearly possessed subject matter jurisdiction over both the underlying suit and the defendants.

Quicknotes

CERTIORARI A discretionary writ issued by a superior court to an inferior court in order to review the lower court's decisions; the Supreme Court's writ ordering such review.

CLASS ACTION A suit commenced by a representative on behalf of an ascertainable group that is too large to appear in court, who shares a commonality of interests and who will benefit from a successful result.

FULL FAITH AND CREDIT Doctrine that a judgment by a court of one state shall be given the same effect in another state.

RES JUDICATA The rule of law that a final judgment by a court precludes subsequent litigation between the parties regarding the same cause of action.

SHAREHOLDER'S DERIVATIVE ACTION Action asserted by a shareholder in order to enforce a cause of action on behalf of the corporation.

SUBJECT MATTER JURISDICTION The authority of the court to hear and decide actions involving a particular type of issue or subject.

Special Problems of Choice of Law, Jurisdiction, and Recognition of Judgments in Divorce, Interstate and International Child Custody, and Decedents' Estates

Quick Reference Rules of Law

11. International Abduction of Children by Spouse.   A court in a nation to which an abused   88
parent abducted her children should conduct an evidentiary hearing before ordering the return
of the children, in order to explore whether the children, if returned to their home country,
would face grave risk of harm and inadequate safeguards for protection. (Van De Sande v. Van
De Sande)

Williams v. State of North Carolina (I)

Ex-spouse (D) v. State (P)

317 U.S. 287 (1942).

NATURE OF CASE: Appeal after conviction for bigamy.

FACT SUMMARY: Williams (D) and Hendrix (D) were granted divorces from their respective spouses in a Nevada court. Williams (D) and Hendrix (D) then married each other and moved back to their former home, North Carolina. The North Carolina court refused to recognize the Nevada divorce decrees and convicted Williams (D) and Hendrix (D) of bigamy.

> 🏛 **RULE OF LAW**
> A divorce granted in state A, on a finding that one spouse was domiciled in state A, must be respected in state B, when state A's finding of domicile is not questioned.

FACTS: Williams (D) and Hendrix (D) were residents of North Carolina. Both moved to Nevada and filed for divorce in a Nevada court against their respective spouses. The defendants in these divorce actions entered no appearance and were not served with process in Nevada. However, service was made by publication in a Nevada newspaper and by personal service of process in North Carolina. Divorces were granted to Williams (D) and Hendrix (D), the Nevada court finding that each was domiciled in Nevada. Williams (D) and Hendrix (D) then married each other in Nevada and moved back to North Carolina. There, Williams (D) and Hendrix (D) were convicted of bigamy on an implicit finding that the Nevada divorce decrees would not be recognized in North Carolina. In affirming the conviction, the North Carolina Supreme Court held that the Nevada divorces need not be recognized, even if the North Carolina court found that Williams (D) and Hendrix (D) had been actually domiciled in Nevada.

ISSUE: Must a divorce granted in state A, on a finding that one spouse was domiciled in state A, be respected in state B, when state A's finding of domicile is not questioned?

HOLDING AND DECISION: (Douglas, J.) Yes. A divorce granted by Nevada, on a finding that one spouse was domiciled there, must be respected in North Carolina, where Nevada's finding of domicile is not questioned by the North Carolina court. The divorce must be respected in North Carolina even though the defendant in the divorce action has neither appeared nor been served with process in Nevada, and though recognition of such a divorce offends the policy of North Carolina. This rule is merely an application of the Full Faith and Credit Clause of the Constitution. If one state were permitted to ignore a divorce in a sister state, even though the requirements of procedural due process were

met in the divorce action, great injustice would result. In the present case, if the court had decided otherwise, Williams (D) and Hendrix (D) would be lawfully married in Nevada but would be bigamists in North Carolina. Their children would be legitimate in one state and illegitimate in another state. Reversed and remanded.

CONCURRENCE: (Frankfurter, J.) North Carolina did not challenge the power of Nevada to declare the marital statue of persons found to be Nevada residents but chose to disrespect the consequences of such power.

DISSENT: (Jackson, J.) There was no conceivable basis of jurisdiction in the Nevada court over the absent spouses.

▶ **ANALYSIS**

The Court explicitly overruled *Haddock v. Haddock*, 201 U.S. 562 (1906), which held that a state does not have jurisdiction over an absent spouse where that state is not the state of the "matrimonial domicile," and where the domiciled spouse has wrongfully left the absent spouse. The Court felt that *Haddock* rested on "immaterial distinctions" and should not be an exception to the rule expounded here. The Court refused in this case to decide whether North Carolina had the right to dispute the Nevada court's procedural finding of domicile as a basis for divorce jurisdiction. This case merely states that North Carolina must accept the Nevada decision where North Carolina does not dispute Nevada's jurisdiction over the proceeding. It was left for a subsequent case, *Williams v. North Carolina*, 325 U.S. 226 (1945), to decide whether a state may reject a sister state's procedural finding of jurisdiction over an action.

■=■

Quicknotes

BIGAMY The criminal offense of willfully and knowingly marrying a second time while knowing that the first marriage is undissolved.

DOMICILE A person's permanent home or principal establishment to which he has an intention of returning when he is absent therefrom.

FULL FAITH AND CREDIT ACT State judicial proceedings shall have such faith and credit given them in every court in the United States as they would in their own state.

IN REM An action against property.

■=■

Estin v. Estin

Wife (P) v. Husband (D)

334 U.S. 541 (1948).

NATURE OF CASE: Suit to enforce payment of alimony.

FACT SUMMARY: Mrs. Estin (P) had received a judgment for permanent alimony from Mr. Estin (D) in a separate maintenance action in New York, where both resided at the time. Mr. Estin (D) subsequently stopped payment after obtaining an ex parte divorce in Nevada which provided for no alimony.

RULE OF LAW
The marital status of the parties is divisible from their rights and obligations thereunder, and a court having jurisdiction over only one element can lawfully adjudicate the issues of that element only.

FACTS: Mr. Estin (D) and Mrs. Estin (P) had been lawfully married in New York but subsequently Mrs. Estin (P) sought and received a judgment of separate maintenance and permanent alimony from Mr. Estin (D) in a New York court in which Mr. Estin (D) made a general appearance. Mr. Estin (D) commenced making the ordered alimony payments and moved his residence to Nevada where he established domicile. He then obtained an ex parte divorce in Nevada, which made no provision for alimony. Mrs. Estin (P) was served by constructive notice, no personal service being made on her. She made no appearance in the Nevada action. Subsequent to the divorce, Mr. Estin (D) ceased making the alimony payments and Mrs. Estin (P) sought to enforce payment. Mr. Estin (D) appeared in the New York proceeding and asserted the Nevada divorce as a defense to further payment. The New York trial and appellate courts denied his defense and he appealed, alleging failure to give full faith and credit.

ISSUE: May a court having jurisdiction over the marital status of the parties also enter a valid judgment concerning the property rights of the respective spouses without jurisdiction over both parties?

HOLDING AND DECISION: (Douglas, J.) No. The decree of divorce was validly entered by the Nevada court and, therefore, it must be given full faith and credit by New York. However, the rights and obligations of the parties are divisible from their marital status and the Nevada court did not have the requisite personal jurisdiction over Mrs. Estin (P) to allow it to adjudicate her rights in that area. The New York judgment of alimony vested in Mrs. Estin (P) an intangible property right over which Nevada could not exercise jurisdiction. A court cannot affect the rights of a creditor without personal jurisdiction over that creditor. This division allows the respective states to exercise domain over that element of the relationship in which they have legitimate interests. Therefore, the parties are divorced but the New York alimony judgment stands and is unaffected by the Nevada decree. Affirmed.

DISSENT: (Frankfurter, J.) Since it is not clear whether New York has held that no "ex parte" divorce decree could determine a prior New York separate maintenance decree or that merely for classification.

DISSENT: (Jackson, J.) If the Nevada judgment is to have full faith and credit, it must have the same effect that a similar New York decree would have.

ANALYSIS

The pronouncement of the divisible nature of a divorce action provided a partial solution to the problem created by "quickie divorce" states.

Quicknotes

ALIMONY Allowances (usually monetary) which husband or wife by court order pays other spouse for maintenance while they are separated, or after they are divorced (permanent alimony), or temporarily, pending a suit for divorce (pendente lite).

EX PARTE A proceeding commenced by one party without providing any opposing parties with notice or which is uncontested by an adverse party.

FULL FAITH AND CREDIT Doctrine that a judgment by a court of one state shall be given the same effect in another state.

Williams v. State of North Carolina (II)

Ex-spouse (D) v. State (P)

325 U.S. 226 (1945).

NATURE OF CASE: Appeal of conviction for bigamy.

FACT SUMMARY: Williams (D) and Hendrix (D) were granted divorces from their respective spouses in a Nevada court. Williams (D) and Hendrix (D) then married each other and moved back to their former home, North Carolina. The North Carolina court refused to recognize the Nevada divorce decrees and convicted Williams (D) and Hendrix (D) of bigamy.

🏛 RULE OF LAW
State B may refuse to recognize a divorce decree granted in state A if state B determines state A's basis of jurisdiction to be unfounded.

FACTS: Williams (D) and Hendrix (D) were residents of North Carolina. Both moved to Nevada and filed for divorce in a Nevada court against their respective spouses. Divorces were granted to Williams (D) and Hendrix (D), the Nevada court finding that each was domiciled in Nevada. Williams (D) and Hendrix (D) then married each other and moved back to North Carolina, where they were indicted for bigamy. Williams (D) and Hendrix (D) were convicted on the ground that they were not domiciled in Nevada when the divorces were granted and that Nevada therefore had no divorce jurisdiction over them.

ISSUE: May state B refuse to recognize a divorce decree granted in state A if state B determines state A's basis of jurisdiction to be unfounded?

HOLDING AND DECISION: (Frankfurter, J.) Yes. A decree of divorce is a conclusive adjudication of everything except the jurisdictional facts upon which it is founded, and domicile is a jurisdictional fact. Thus, North Carolina may refuse to recognize the Nevada divorces if the North Carolina court determines that Nevada erred in its finding of domicile. However, the Full Faith and Credit Clause demands that the determination of jurisdiction by one state be given great weight in a sister state. Such a jurisdictional finding may be rejected only if the party urging its rejection can overcome the burden of proof and can provide ample evidence of lack of jurisdiction. In the present case, the North Carolina trial court appropriately charged the jury that Nevada's finding of domicile was prima facie evidence of such domicile, but was not conclusive. Acting under that standard of proof, North Carolina had the right to reject Nevada's finding of domicile. Affirmed.

▶ ANALYSIS

Because North Carolina did not question Nevada's finding that Williams (D) and Hendrix (D) were domiciled in Nevada at the time of their divorces, the first *Williams* case ruled that the divorces granted to them by Nevada must be respected in North Carolina. However, in the second *Williams* case, the Supreme Court addressed an issue that was not present in the prior appeal, namely, whether North Carolina had the power "to refuse full faith and credit to Nevada divorce decrees because, contrary to the findings of the Nevada court, North Carolina finds that no bona fide domicile was acquired in Nevada." The Court ruled that North Carolina had such power. The second *Williams* case raises the question presented in *Colby v. Colby*, 78 Nev. 150, 369 P.2d 1019 (1962), *cert. denied*, 371 U.S. 888 (1962), in which a Maryland court had found that a Nevada finding of divorce jurisdiction was improper and the divorce was invalid. Despite Maryland's decision, the Nevada court upheld the divorce when its validity was questioned there. Thus, the divorce was valid in Nevada and invalid in Maryland, a result which seems to thwart the purpose of the Full Faith and Credit Clause, as discussed in the first *Williams* case.

Quicknotes

BIGAMY The criminal offense of willfully and knowingly marrying a second time while knowing that the first marriage is undissolved.

DOMICILE A person's permanent home or principal establishment to which he has an intention of returning when he is absent therefrom.

FULL FAITH AND CREDIT ACT State judicial proceedings shall have such faith and credit given them in every court in the United States as they would in their own state.

PRIMA FACIE EVIDENCE Evidence presented by a party that is sufficient, in the absence of contradictory evidence, to support the fact or issue for which it is offered.

Sherrer v. Sherrer

Ex-husband (D) v. Ex-wife (P)

334 U.S. 343 (1948).

NATURE OF CASE: Collateral attack on divorce decree granted by sister state.

FACT SUMMARY: Mrs. Sherrer (P) left her home and husband in Massachusetts to obtain a divorce in Florida. Mr. Sherrer (D) appeared personally in that proceeding in which all issues, including domicile, were litigated. He now seeks to void the decree in Massachusetts for lack of Florida jurisdiction.

🏛 **RULE OF LAW**
A decree of divorce granted by a sister state is not subject to attack and must be given full faith and credit where such attack would not prevail in the rendering state because of res judicata.

FACTS: Mr. (D) and Mrs. (P) Sherrer were domiciled in Massachusetts during their marriage. Mrs. Sherrer (P) went to Florida where she obtained a divorce in a proceeding in which Mr. Sherrer (D) personally appeared and litigated all issues including the validity of her domicile. She subsequently moved back to Massachusetts where Mr. Sherrer (D) sought to void the divorce as having been granted by Florida without proper jurisdiction since he contended she was never properly domiciled in Florida.

ISSUE: Must full faith and credit be given to the divorce decree of a sister state where such decree was granted after personal appearances by both parties and litigation of all issues including jurisdiction?

HOLDING AND DECISION: (Vinson, C.J.) Yes. The issue of domicile must be resolved by judicial determination. But once that issue has been litigated and determined it is as subject to the doctrine of res judicata as any other issue. Where a divorce has been granted by one state where the issue of domicile has been litigated by all parties, as in this case, as long as that decree is not subject to collateral attack in the rendering state, it is immune from such attack elsewhere. Mr. Sherrer (D) appeared personally and was represented by counsel in the Florida proceeding. If he felt the trial court erred, the appellate process of that state was available to him. Since he did not appeal at that time, the decree thus entered must be given full faith and credit in Massachusetts. Reversed.

DISSENT: (Frankfurter, J.) The majority understands the Full Faith and Credit Clause to give states which offer bargain-counter divorces constitutional power to control the social policy governing domestic relations of the many states which do not. The state has an interest the family relations of its citizens vastly different from the interest it has in an ordinary commercial transaction. Therefore, the constitutional power of a state to determine the marriage status of its citizens should not be deemed foreclosed by a proceeding between the parties in another state, even though in other types of controversy, considerations making it desirable to put an end to litigation might foreclose the parties themselves from reopening the dispute.

▶ **ANALYSIS**

The principle of this case has been extended to situations where the defendant spouse has not personally appeared but has been represented in a general appearance by a local attorney. In such cases, full faith and credit has been granted even where no issues were litigated if they could have been. However, where the attorney representing the defendant spouse is controlled by the plaintiff spouse or where consent has been obtained by misrepresentation, full faith and credit has been denied.

■=■

Quicknotes

COLLATERAL ATTACK A proceeding initiated in order to challenge the integrity of a previous judgment.

DOMICILE A person's permanent home or principal establishment to which he has an intention of returning when he is absent therefrom.

FULL FAITH AND CREDIT Doctrine that a judgment by a court of one state shall be given the same effect in another state.

RES JUDICATA The rule of law that a final judgment by a court precludes subsequent litigation between the parties regarding the same cause of action.

■=■

Rosenstiel v. Rosenstiel

Husband (P) v. Wife (D)

N.Y. Ct. App., 16 N.Y.2d 64, 209 N.E.2d 709 (1965).

NATURE OF CASE: Appeal from dismissal of an action to annul a marriage.

FACT SUMMARY: Husband (P), a New York resident, sought to annul his marriage to wife (D) on grounds that her bilateral, consensual Mexican divorce from her first husband was invalid.

🏛 RULE OF LAW
Bilateral Mexican divorces should be recognized as not offending the public policy of New York.

FACTS: Husband (P), a New York resident, sought to annul his marriage to wife (D), a New York resident. Wife (D) was first married to Kaufman. Kaufman, a New York resident, obtained a Mexican divorce from wife (D) in 1954. He spent one day in Juarez, where he signed the municipal register, the official book of city residents, and petitioned in the court there for divorce. Wife (D) appeared through her attorney, and she admitted Kaufman's allegations of ill treatment. The divorce was granted the same day and is recognized as valid by the Republic of Mexico. Husband (P) contended that the Mexican divorce was invalid and that, therefore, wife (D) was incompetent to contract their 1956 marriage. The trial court annulled the marriage. The Appellate division reversed and dismissed the complaint. Husband (P) appealed.

ISSUE: Should New York recognize bilateral Mexican divorces as not offending that state's public policy?

HOLDING AND DECISION: (Bergan, J.) Yes. Bilateral Mexican divorces should be recognized as not offending the public policy of New York. In cases where the parties have had no personal contact with the foreign jurisdiction, the divorce has not been recognized. Here, Kaufman was physically within the jurisdiction, personally before the court, "with the usual incidents and the implicit consequences of voluntary submission to foreign sovereignty." He did establish at least a statutory residence there. Kaufman also carried with him the legal incidents of the marriage. Additionally, the wife's (D) appearance through her attorney gave further support to an acquired jurisdiction over the marriage as a legal entity. "[A]lmost universally jurisdiction is acquired by physical and personal submission to judicial authority." Accordingly, the divorce must be recognized and the appeal denied. Affirmed.

CONCURRENCE IN PART: (Desmond, C.J.) Foreign divorces should only be recognized when they do not offend the state's public policy. But a Mexican divorce decree which is blatantly consensual is against New York public policy. As to sister states with short residency periods,

the Full Faith and Credit Clause of the Constitution requires recognition of their divorce decrees, but nothing requires the same with foreign divorce decrees. Therefore, New York should prospectively refuse to recognize consensual Mexican divorces. Past Mexican divorces should be recognized only because the reality of the situation prohibits invalidating tens of thousands of divorces gotten by New York residents in Mexico.

▶ *ANALYSIS*

New York is the only state which has recognized bilateral, consensual Mexican divorces. The court may have simply been trying to avoid New York's archaic divorce law which provided only one ground for divorce, adultery. New York never recognized either ex parte, unilateral Mexican divorces or Mexican "mail order" divorces. New York liberalized its divorce law in 1966.

■═■

Quicknotes

PUBLIC POLICY Policy administered by the state with respect to the health, safety and morals of its people in accordance with common notions of fairness and decency.

■═■

Chambers v. Ormiston

Spouse (P) v. Spouse (P)

R.I. Sup. Ct., 935 A.2d 956 (2007).

NATURE OF CASE: Certified question to the Rhode Island Supreme Court from the family court.

FACT SUMMARY: Two female Rhode Island residents were married in Massachusetts. Subsequently, they petitioned the Rhode Island Family Court for dissolution of the marriage.

⚖ RULE OF LAW
Rhode Island's family court does not have subject matter jurisdiction to hear a petition for dissolution of a same sex marriage because the term "marriage," at the time the legislature created the family court in 1961, only referred to marriage as being between a man and a woman.

FACTS: Chambers (P) and Ormiston (D), Rhode Island residents, traveled to Massachusetts in 2004 and were married in a ceremony in that state. In 2006, both parties petitioned the Rhode Island Family Court for a divorce. The family court then certified a question to the Rhode Island Supreme Court as to whether the family court had subject matter jurisdiction to grant a petition for divorce with respect to same sex couples.

ISSUE: Does Rhode Island's family court have subject matter jurisdiction to hear a petition for dissolution of a same sex marriage when the term "marriage," at the time the legislature created the family court in 1961, only referred to marriage as being between a man and a woman?

HOLDING AND DECISION: (Robinson, J.) No. Rhode Island's family court does not have subject matter jurisdiction to hear a petition for dissolution of a same sex marriage because the term "marriage," at the time the legislature created the family court in 1961, only referred to marriage as being between a man and a woman. To determine whether the family court has power to hear a divorce petition of a same sex couple, validly married in Massachusetts, the court must review the definition of the term "marriage" as it was defined when the state legislature created the family court in 1961. G.L. 1956 Section 8-10-3(a) provides the family court to hear "all petitions for divorce from the bond of marriage." In determining the intent of the legislature, it is appropriate to review contemporaneous dictionaries. In 1961, most dictionaries regarded marriage as between one man and one woman. The legislature has not done anything since 1961 to change that definition. Accordingly, the family court has no jurisdiction to hear a petition for a divorce of a same sex couple. If there is to be a remedy here, it should come from the legislature and not the courts. Certified question is answered in the negative.

DISSENT: (Suttell, J.) The court's opinion is correct in that legal recognition of same-sex marriages in Rhode Island should be determined by the state legislature and not the courts. However, the validity of the parties' marriage here is not in dispute nor is it challenged by either party. There is no question the parties were married legally in Massachusetts. There is nothing in the 1961 statute that would preclude the family court from hearing their divorce petition. The only question here is whether the family court may hear a divorce petition from a couple validly married in another state, not whether same-sex couples may marry in Rhode Island under this state's marriage laws. Because the couple is domiciled in Rhode Island, this is the only forum where they can seek a divorce.

▶ ANALYSIS

This was a three to two decision by the Rhode Island Supreme Court. The one point all of the justices agreed upon was that the decision to allow same-sex couples to marry in Rhode Island should come from the state legislature. Since this decision, no less than seven different bills have been entered in the Rhode Island state legislature to recognize either same-sex marriage or civil unions. As of July 2010, none of those bills had passed.

Quicknotes

DOMICILE A person's permanent home or principal establishment to which he has an intention of returning when he is absent therefrom.

SUBJECT MATTER JURISDICTION The authority of the court to hear and decide actions involving a particular type of issue or subject.

Welch-Doden v. Roberts

Mother (P) v. Father (D)

Ariz. Ct. App., 202 Ariz. 201, 42 P.3d 1166 (2002).

NATURE OF CASE: Appeal of dismissal for lack of jurisdiction in child custody case.

FACT SUMMARY: Four months after moving to Arizona, mother (P) files for divorce and custody, and after that, father (D) files for divorce and custody in Oklahoma. Arizona trial court determines that Oklahoma has jurisdiction. Oklahoma then awards custody to father (D) in Oklahoma.

RULE OF LAW

(1) The Uniform Child Custody Jurisdiction and Enforcement Act (UCCJEA) provides that "home state" jurisdiction is the last state the child resided in for six consecutive months at any time within six months of the filing for custody.
(2) The best interests of the child are not properly in jurisdictional analysis.
(3) First-in-time filing in a non-home state does not defeat jurisdiction of the home state.

FACTS: A child was born in Oklahoma in April 1999 to Melissa Welch-Doden (P) and Terry Welch-Doden (D). The family moved a lot. The child resided in Oklahoma seven and a half months until December 1999. The child then resided in Arizona for three months from December 1999 through March 2000. The child returned to Oklahoma for the next six months from March 2000 through September 2000. At that point, the mother moved with the child back to Arizona for four months, at the end of which, on January 25, 2001, Melissa (P) filed a petition for dissolution and child custody in Arizona. Terry (D) filed for divorce and custody in Oklahoma shortly thereafter. After conferring with the Oklahoma court, the Arizona court dismissed the action on grounds that Oklahoma was child's home state under the UCCJEA. Melissa (P) filed petition for special action.

ISSUE:

(1) Does the UCCJEA provide that "home state" jurisdiction is the last state the child resided in for six consecutive months at any time within six months of the filing for custody?
(2) Are the best interests of the child properly considered in jurisdictional analysis?
(3) Does first-in-time filing in a non-home state defeat jurisdiction of the home state?

HOLDING AND DECISION: (Barker, J.)

(1) Yes. The UCCJEA provides that "home state" jurisdiction is the last state the child resided in for six consecutive months at any time within six months of the

filing for custody. The primary purpose of the UCCJEA is to establish the certainty of home state jurisdiction by avoiding jurisdictional competition and conflict that comes from court inquiry into substantive review of subjective factors, such as "best interests," for purposes of determining initial jurisdiction. In order to interpret the UCCJEA in a way that promotes the purposes intended by the drafters, the definition of home state jurisdiction has to be expanded to consist of the state in which the child resided for six months before commencement of the child custody proceeding, not necessarily immediately preceding the commencement of the proceeding.

(2) No. The best interests of the child are not properly considered in jurisdictional analysis. The drafters of the UCCJEA expressly sought to eliminate jurisdictional disputes that resulted when "best interests" was used to determine initial jurisdiction, because different jurisdictions could arrive at different conclusions regarding "best interests," and therefore arrive at different results regarding jurisdiction.

(3) No. First-in-time filing in a non-home state does not defeat jurisdiction of the home state. First-in-time filing must be in a state having jurisdiction substantially in conformity with the law, and because Oklahoma had home state jurisdiction, Arizona did not have jurisdiction substantially in conformity. Affirmed.

ANALYSIS

This case is often cited by other jurisdictions dealing with the UCCJEA. The fact that at all times during every move, the child was with his mother, was expressly dismissed by the court as not having bearing on the jurisdictional issue, which, when considered outside the narrow issue of jurisdiction and in light of the larger custody issue, might go against the best interests of the child under current family law rules.

Quicknotes

DISSOLUTION Annulment or termination of a formal or legal bond, tie or contract.

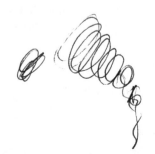

Grahm v. Superior Court

Father (P) v. Mother (D)

Cal. Ct. App., 132 Cal. App. 4th 1193, 34 Cal. Rptr. 3d 270 (2005).

NATURE OF CASE: Appeal of denial of custody modification request.

FACT SUMMARY: Mr. Grahm (P) sought to modify custody in California while the children and Mrs. Grahm (D) lived in New York. The California trial court declined to exercise jurisdiction.

🏛 RULE OF LAW
A California court has exclusive, continuing jurisdiction over a child custody determination that originated in California until a court in the state determines that neither the child, nor the child and one parent have significant connections with the state and that substantial evidence is no longer available in the state concerning the child's care, protection, training, and personal relationships.

FACTS: Mr. Grahm (P) and Mrs. Grahm (D) were married and divorced in California. They had two children who were born in California. As part of the divorce decree, the court granted joint custody to both parents, and primary physical custody to Mrs. Grahm (D). One month before entry of the judgment, Mrs. Grahm (D) moved, with Mr. Grahm's (P) consent, to New York. Mr. Grahm (P) then sought to modify custody in California. The California trial court declined to exercise jurisdiction.

ISSUE: Does a California court have exclusive, continuing jurisdiction over a child custody determination that originated in California until a court in the state determines that neither the child, nor the child and one parent have significant connections with the state and that substantial evidence is no longer available in the state concerning the child's care, protection, training, and personal relationships?

HOLDING AND DECISION: (Hastings, J.) Yes. A California court has exclusive, continuing jurisdiction over a child custody determination that originated in California until a court in the state determines that neither the child, nor the child and one parent have significant connections with the state and that substantial evidence is no longer available in the state concerning the child's care, protection, training, and personal relationships. The out-of-state residency of the children and Mrs. Grahm (D) does not terminate a significant connection with California, as long as a parent continues to exercise visitation rights in California. Case law interpreting "significant connections" as the term applied to the old Uniform Child Custody Jurisdiction Act (UCCJEA) also applies to the new Uniform Child Custody Jurisdiction and Enforcement Act, because the new act retained a lot of the original language of the old, and because the drafters of the new act had the same goal as the old regarding modification jurisdiction, which was to retain modification jurisdiction in the decreeing state until all of the connection between the parent and child is lost. The California legislature meant to preserve in the new act the construction of "significant connection" by case law as applied to the old act. In addition, it is not clear that the lower court determined that substantial evidence is no longer available in California concerning the child's care, protection, training, and personal relationships. California trial court reversed and Mr. Grahm's petition granted.

▶ ANALYSIS

It could be argued that by applying case law that applied to the UCCJEA's predecessor to the UCCJEA, the California appeals court attempted to avoid an undesired change in the law allowing California to retain jurisdiction even without significant connections between the state and the mother. In addition, it could be argued that the appeals court stretched to find that the lower court judge failed to determine that substantial evidence regarding the children's welfare was no longer available in California. The lower court judge said: "Neither the child nor the child and one parent nor the child and a person acting as a parent ha[s] a significant connection with this state and that substantial evidence is no longer available in this state concerning the child's care, protection, training and personal relationship. I am making that determination today." The statement seems clear, despite the appeals court's holding to the contrary.

■▬■

Quicknotes

JURISDICTION The authority of a court to hear and declare judgment in respect to a particular matter.

■▬■

Lisa Miller-Jenkins v. Janet Miller-Jenkins

Spouse (P) v. Spouse (D)

Vt. Sup. Ct., 912 A.2d 951 (2006), *cert. denied*, 550 U.S. 918 (2007).

NATURE OF CASE: Appeal from family court decision in favor of defendant.

FACT SUMMARY: Lisa (P) and Janet (D) were married in Vermont. After Lisa (P) conceived, the couple lived with their minor child in Vermont for one year. Lisa then filed for a dissolution in Vermont.

🏛 RULE OF LAW
Under the federal Parental Kidnapping Prevention Act (PKPA), where one state has valid jurisdiction over a child custody matter pursuant to the statutory language, another state lacks jurisdiction to hear the same matter as long as the case remains pending in the first state.

FACTS: Lisa (P) and Janet (D) originally lived in Virginia. In 2000, the parties traveled to Vermont and entered into a valid civil union in accordance with the laws of Vermont. In 2001, Lisa received artificial insemination and gave birth in April 2002. Four months later, the parties moved to Vermont and lived there for just over one year. The parties separated in September 2003 and Lisa (P) moved back to Virginia with the minor child, which was given the designation of IMJ by the court. In November 2003, Lisa (P) filed for a dissolution of the civil union in Vermont. In the complaint, Lisa (P) listed IMJ as the "biological or adoptive" child of the civil union. The family court issued a temporary order awarding Lisa (P) temporary legal and physical responsibility of IMJ and awarded Janet visitation rights. Lisa (P) did not allow visitation but instead filed a petition in Virginia to establish IMJ's parentage. The Virginia family court found Janet (D) had no parental rights on grounds Vermont's civil unions laws were invalid under Virginia law. That order was on appeal to the Virginia Court of Appeals. The Vermont family court refused to give full faith and credit to the Virginia family court's decision regarding Janet's (D) lack of parental rights. Lisa (D) appealed the family court's decision that Janet (D) had parental rights.

ISSUE: Under the federal Parental Kidnapping Prevention Act (PKPA), where one state has valid jurisdiction over a child custody matter pursuant to the statutory language, does another state lack jurisdiction to hear the same matter as long as the case remains pending in the first state?

HOLDING AND DECISION: (Dooley, J.) Yes. Under the federal Parental Kidnapping Prevention Act (PKPA), where one state has valid jurisdiction over a child custody matter pursuant to the statutory language, another state lacks jurisdiction to hear the same matter as long as the case remains pending in the first state. The purpose of the

PKPA is to maintain jurisdiction in the state that entered the original decree and to discourage parental abduction for the purpose of obtaining a more favorable ruling in a different state. The PKPA applies to custody and visitation determinations. Lisa (P) filed her first case in Vermont before she filed her second case in Virginia. Under the PKPA, this court must determine if Vermont had jurisdiction in accordance with the PKPA. If it did, then Virginia had no jurisdiction to hear the matter. Under the PKPA, to have jurisdiction, one way is for Vermont to be the child's home state within six months before the proceeding began, the child is currently absent from the state, and one party to the action still lives in the state. Each of those conditions is present here. Lisa (P), Janet (D) and IMJ all lived in the state six months before the case began. IMJ is absent from the state and Janet (D) continues to reside here. Under the PKPA, the court must also have jurisdiction under the local Uniform Child Custody Jurisdiction Act. The language in that Vermont statute is identical to the federal PKPA. Jurisdiction under that local statute is also proper. Because Vermont had valid jurisdiction at the time Lisa (P) filed her action in Virginia, the Virginia court did not have jurisdiction to hear the case pursuant to Section 1738(g) of the PKPA. Lisa's (P) reliance on the Defense of Marriage Act (DOMA) is improper. DOMA states that no state shall be required to give effect to a judicial proceeding in another state regarding the relationships between people of the same sex. However, DOMA does not demand or require one state to give full faith and credit to the decision of a court in another state. Vermont has jurisdiction in the first instance, and no language in DOMA forces Vermont to recognize the Virginia court's decision. The civil union in this case was valid and the PKPA holds that Virginia had no jurisdiction over the matter where Vermont had valid jurisdiction over the case. Affirmed and remanded.

▶ ANALYSIS

As will be seen in the related appellate case from Virginia, *Janet Miller-Jenkins v. Lisa Miller-Jenkins*, Va. App., 637 S.E.2d 330 (2006), the Virginia Court of Appeals agrees with the Vermont Supreme Court and finds the Virginia family court did not have jurisdiction to hear the case pursuant to the federal PKPA.

Quicknotes

PARENTAL KIDNAPPING PREVENTION ACT 28 U.S.C. § 1738A Federal law governing the enforcement and modification of foreign decrees and the treatment of concurrent

Continued on next page.

proceedings. Only custody determinations made consistent with its provisions are to be given full faith and credit by states. It preempts conflicting state law and requires that a custody determination be made in the child's home state.

UNIFORM CHILD CUSTODY JURISDICTION ACT A uniform law adopted in all states to deal with multi-state child custody and visitation disputes. Enacted to deter parental kidnapping, it generally recognizes jurisdiction in a child's "home state."

■━■

Janet Miller-Jenkins v. Lisa Miller-Jenkins

Spouse (D) v. Spouse (P)

Va. App., 637 S.E.2d 330 (2006).

NATURE OF CASE: Appeal from family court decision in favor of plaintiff.

FACT SUMMARY: Lisa (P) and Janet (D) were married in Vermont. After Lisa (P) conceived, the couple lived with their minor child in Vermont for one year. Lisa (P) filed for a dissolution in Vermont and then filed a subsequent petition for parental rights in Virginia.

RULE OF LAW

Under the federal Parental Kidnapping Prevention Act (PKPA), a state must give full faith and credit to child custody and visitation determinations made by another state that validly exercised jurisdiction in accordance with the PKPA.

FACTS: Lisa (P) and Janet (D) originally lived in Virginia. In 2000, the parties traveled to Vermont and entered into a valid civil union in accordance with the laws of Vermont. In 2001, Lisa received artificial insemination and gave birth in April 2002. Four months later, the parties moved to Vermont and lived there for just over one year. The parties separated in September 2003 and Lisa (P) moved back to Virginia with the minor child, which was given the designation of IMJ by the court. In November 2003, Lisa (P) filed for a dissolution of the civil union in Vermont. In the complaint, Lisa (P) listed IMJ as the "biological or adoptive" child of the civil union. The family court issued a temporary order awarding Lisa (P) temporary legal and physical responsibility of IMJ and awarded Janet visitation rights. Lisa (P) did not allow visitation but instead filed a petition in Virginia to establish IMJ's parentage. The Virginia family court found Janet (D) had no parental rights on grounds Vermont's civil unions laws were invalid under Virginia law. The Vermont family court refused to give full faith and credit to the Virginia family court's decision regarding Janet's (D) lack of parental rights. The Vermont Supreme Court affirmed that decision. In Virginia, Janet (D) appealed on the grounds the Virginia family court failed to recognize that the PKPA bars jurisdiction in Virginia.

ISSUE: Under the federal Parental Kidnapping Prevention Act (PKPA), must a state give full faith and credit to child custody and visitation determinations made by another state that validly exercised jurisdiction in accordance with the PKPA?

HOLDING AND DECISION: (Willis, Jr., J.) Yes. Under the federal Parental Kidnapping Prevention Act (PKPA), a state must give full faith and credit to child custody and visitation determinations made by another

state that validly exercised jurisdiction in accordance with the PKPA. Under the PKPA, Vermont had jurisdiction because the parties lived there within six months of the case being filed in Vermont, IMJ was absent from the state and Janet (D) remained in the state. Accordingly, jurisdiction was proper in Vermont, and the Virginia family court had no jurisdiction to hear this case while the matter was still pending in Vermont. Lisa (P) contends the Vermont court improperly determined that Janet was a parent. However, Lisa's (P) own complaint in Vermont stated IMJ was the "biological or adoptive" child of the civil union. The custody and visitation rights were validly determined by the Vermont court and this court cannot reconsider them here. Lisa's (P) argument that DOMA trumps the PKPA is also incorrect. There is no language that DOMA sought to repeal the PKPA. Without express intent by Congress to do so, this court will not infer that DOMA repealed portions of the PKPA. DOMA allows one state to deny the recognition of same sex marriages by another state. That is not the issue here. The only question before this court is whether, under the PKPA, Virginia can deny Vermont's judicial decisions full faith and credit. This court cannot do so. Lisa's (P) own choice of Vermont as the initial place to file her petition thus precludes Virginia from hearing the same claim. Lastly, Virginia's Marriage Affirmation Act, which parrots the federal DOMA act, is preempted by the PKPA. Reversed and remanded with instruction to give full faith and credit to the orders of the Vermont court.

ANALYSIS

The significance of this decision was the court's finding that the PKPA was the controlling federal statute and that it was not trumped by DOMA. As the court noted, the issue here was not recognition of civil unions or same sex marriages, but rather a jurisdictional question over the care and custody of a child.

■═■

Quicknotes

FEDERAL QUESTION JURISDICTION The authority of the federal courts to hear and determine in the first instance matters pertaining to the federal Constitution, federal law, or treaties of the United States.

REMOVAL Petition by a defendant to move the case to another court.

■═■

Van De Sande v. Van De Sande

Father (P) v. Mother (D)

431 F.3d 567 (7th Cir. 2005).

NATURE OF CASE: Appeal of summary judgment.

FACT SUMMARY: Jennifer Van De Sande (D) refused to return to Belgium, where she lived with her abusive husband, and kept her children with her. Davy Van De Sande (P) sought return of the children under the Hague Convention's provisions against child abductions. A federal district court granted summary judgment for Davy (P).

🏛️ **RULE OF LAW**
A court in a nation to which an abused parent abducted her children should conduct an evidentiary hearing before ordering the return of the children, in order to explore whether the children, if returned to their home country, would face grave risk of harm and inadequate safeguards for protection.

FACTS: Davy Van De Sande (P) and his mother physically and verbally abused his wife and daughter while they lived in Belgium. When they came to the United States to visit Jennifer Van De Sande's (D) family, Jennifer (D) decided not to return to Belgium and to keep her children in the United States. Davy (P) threatened to kill her, the children, and her whole family. Jennifer's (D) father called the police and had Davy (P) removed from the house. Davy (P) returned to Belgium and petitioned a court there for return of his children, pursuant to the Hague Convention's provisions against child abductions. Jennifer (D), meanwhile, petitioned a U.S. federal court to excuse return, on grounds that return would place the children at grave risk of physical or psychological harm. The district court granted summary judgment for Davy (P), on the ground that there was no indication that the Belgian legal system could not or would not protect the children.

ISSUE: Should a court in a nation to which an abused parent abducted her children conduct an evidentiary hearing before ordering the return of the children, in order to explore whether the children, if returned to their home country, would face grave risk of harm and inadequate safeguards for protection?

HOLDING AND DECISION: (Posner, J.) Yes. A court in a nation to which an abused parent abducted her children should conduct an evidentiary hearing before ordering the return of the children, in order to explore whether the children, if returned to their home country, would face grave risk of harm and inadequate safeguards for protection. The gravity of a risk involves not only the probability of harm, but also the magnitude of the harm if the harm occurs, and the probability that Davy (P) or his mother might cause actual physical injury to the children is not negligible. The court must be satisfied that the children will in fact, not just in theory, be protected if returned to their abuser's custody. Until it is so satisfied, the children must be kept protected. In child abuse cases, the balance shifts against "return plus conditions," and even though comity mandates a narrow interpretation of the "grave risk of harm" defense, the safety of the children is paramount, and an evidentiary hearing is justified. Reversed and remanded.

▶ **ANALYSIS**

The Hague Convention requires the prompt return of a child abducted to another country. The exception in this case required Jennifer (D) to show by clear and convincing evidence that return would cause grave harm to the child, and that the Belgian court could not protect the child. Given that her only evidence was affidavits by her and her family, she may not have met her burden.

Quicknotes

COMITY A rule pursuant to which courts in one state give deference to the statutes and judicial decisions of the courts of another state.

EVIDENTIARY HEARING Hearing pertaining to the evidence of the case.

HAGUE SERVICE CONVENTION Multilateral treaty governing service of process in foreign jurisdictions.

SUMMARY JUDGMENT Judgment rendered by a court in response to a motion made by one of the parties, claiming that the lack of a question of material fact in respect to an issue warrants disposition of the issue without consideration by the jury.

Conflicts Between Federal and State Law

Quick Reference Rules of Law

Osborn v. Bank of the United States

State auditors (D) v. Federal Commissioners (P)

22 U.S. (9 Wheat.) 738 (1824).

NATURE OF CASE: Review of injunction ordering return of state tax levy on federal entity.

FACT SUMMARY: Osborn (D) contended that the federal judiciary lacked jurisdiction to hear a case involving the Bank of the United States (P).

🏛 RULE OF LAW
The federal judiciary has jurisdiction coextensive with that of Congress.

FACTS: In contravention to a federal court ruling, Osborn (D), a state auditor for Ohio, went to the Ohio branch of the Bank of the United States (P) and forcibly removed a tax levy. Federal commissioners responded by imprisoning Osborn (D). The federal court ordered the money returned. Osborn (D) appealed, contending that the court lacked subject-matter jurisdiction.

ISSUE: Does the federal judiciary have jurisdiction coextensive with that of Congress?

HOLDING AND DECISION: (Marshall, C.J.) Yes. The federal judiciary has jurisdiction coextensive with that of Congress. Whether the Bank (P) falls within this coextensive jurisdiction depends on the answer to these questions: (1) did Congress give such jurisdiction, and (2) could Congress constitutionally do so? The answer to the first question must be in the affirmative, as the statute creating the Bank (P) gives it standing to sue and be sued in federal court. The question then becomes whether such an enactment is constitutional. Osborn (D) contended that it was not because an action involving the Bank (P) may involve issues of state law, and thus not arise under federal law, as federal cases constitutionally must if diversity is absent. This Court finds this analysis flawed; if the presence of a state law issue could always defeat the presence of a federal question, virtually no cases could be heard in federal court. Rather, the better rule is that federal courts have jurisdiction coextensive with that of Congress. Just as Congress can regulate in matters involving state law, federal courts can hear matters involving state law. Here, since the Bank (D) is a creature of federal law, suits involving it are properly in federal court. Affirmed.

DISSENT: (Johnson, J.) Congress may not create federal subject matter jurisdiction merely by conferring the right to sue in federal court; rather, the cause of action asserted must arise under federal law.

▶ ANALYSIS

The present case has a rather important prologue. Originally, Maryland had levied a tax on the Bank of the United States (P). The Supreme Court, in *McCulloch v. Maryland*, 17 U.S. 316 (1819), held that a state had no such power to tax the federal Bank (P), using the now-famous phrase, "The power to tax is the power to destroy."

Quicknotes

SUBJECT MATTER JURISDICTION A court's ability to adjudicate a specific category of cases based on the subject matter of the dispute.

Louisville & Nashville R. Co. v. Mottley

Railroad (D) v. Injured passenger (P)

211 U.S. 149 (1908).

NATURE OF CASE: Review of award of specific performance of contract.

FACT SUMMARY: Mottley (P) brought an action in federal court because the main defense thereto was based on federal law.

🏛 RULE OF LAW
That an anticipated defense to an action is based on federal law is insufficient to confer federal jurisdiction.

FACTS: As part of a personal injury settlement, Louisville & Nashville Railroad Co. (D) agreed to give Mottley (P) free lifetime railroad passes. In 1906, Congress enacted legislation which, among other things, forbade railroads from giving free passes. Louisville (D) stopped providing free passes to Mottley (P), who brought an action for specific performance in federal court. The court of appeals entered an order of specific performance, and Louisville (D) petitioned for certiorari.

ISSUE: Is an anticipated defense to an action based on federal law sufficient to confer federal jurisdiction?

HOLDING AND DECISION: (Moody, J.) No. That an anticipated defense to an action is based on federal law is insufficient to confer federal jurisdiction. For federal question jurisdiction to exist, an action must "arise under" the Constitution or federal law. It seems clear that this refers to the cause of action asserted by the plaintiff, not any possible defense asserted by the defendant. Federal question jurisdiction did not exist. Here, Mottley's (P) cause of action was based on state contract law and had no federal dimension. Consequently, Louisville's (D) anticipated federal-law defense did not in itself confer federal jurisdiction. Reversed and dismissed.

▶ ANALYSIS

Jurisdiction is the one defense that is never waived. In this particular lawsuit, the issue was never addressed in the courts below or even by the parties at the Supreme Court level; the Court raised the issue sua sponte. This situation presents a potential trap for the unwary practitioner; a plaintiff attorney may find his federal case dismissed for lack of jurisdiction years after he has filed it, and after the statute of limitations has run for filing in state court.

Quicknotes

CERTIORARI A discretionary writ issued by a superior court to an inferior court in order to review the lower court's decisions; the Supreme Court's writ ordering such review.

JURISDICTION The authority of a court to hear and declare judgment in respect to a particular matter.

SPECIFIC PERFORMANCE An equitable remedy whereby the court requires the parties to perform their obligations pursuant to a contract.

SUA SPONTE An action taken by the court by its own motion and without the suggestion of one of the parties.

Grable & Sons Metal Products, Inc., Petitioner v. Darue Engineering & Manufacturing

Former Land Owner (P) v. Current Land Owner (D)

544 U.S. 960 (2005).

NATURE OF CASE: Appeal from Sixth Circuit Court of Appeals in favor of defendant.

FACT SUMMARY: The Internal Revenue Service (IRS) seized land owned by Grable (P) to satisfy a delinquent federal tax. Darue (D) acquired a quitclaim deed to the property at a federal tax sale. Grable (P) brought suit alleging it did not receive proper notice of the seizure.

🏛 RULE OF LAW
In cases that lack a federal cause of action, federal question jurisdiction may still exist over state law claims that implicate significant federal issues if such jurisdiction will not distort the division of labor between the state and federal courts.

FACTS: In 1994, the IRS seized property owned by Grable (P) to satisfy an outstanding federal tax bill. Darue (D) subsequently purchased the property at a federal tax sale and received a quitclaim deed from the federal government. Five years later, Grable (P) brought a quiet title action in state court against Darue (D) alleging that the IRS failed to follow the precise statutory mandate for notification of the seizure of property. Grable (P) argued the statute required personal service of the notification, not via certified mail. Darue (D) removed the case to federal court on the ground the case depended on an interpretation of a federal tax statute. The district court agreed, denied Grable's (P) request for a remand, and granted Darue (D) summary judgment on the merits. The Sixth Circuit affirmed. The U.S. Supreme Court granted certiorari on the jurisdictional question alone to determine if federal question jurisdiction requires the presence of a federal cause of action.

ISSUE: In cases that lack a federal cause of action, may federal question jurisdiction still exist over state law claims that implicate significant federal issues if such jurisdiction will not distort the division of labor between the state and federal courts?

HOLDING AND DECISION: (Souter, J.) Possibly. In cases that lack a federal cause of action, federal question jurisdiction may still exist over state law claims that implicate significant federal issues if such jurisdiction will not distort the division of labor between the state and federal courts. Darue (D) was entitled to removal if the case could have been brought in federal court initially. Normally, a federal cause of action or diversity is necessary to invoke subject matter jurisdiction in federal court. This Court has recognized another avenue for federal question jurisdiction. In certain cases, federal question jurisdiction will lie over state law claims that implicate significant federal issues. However, granting jurisdiction to such cases must not upset the balance over the division of labor between state and federal courts. Here, the case clearly calls for federal jurisdiction. The only undisputed legal issue is the interpretation of a federal tax statute. The government has a strong interest in prompt collection of taxes. Moreover, because the state law claim is a rare, quiet title claim based on a federal seizure of property, granting jurisdiction will not distort the balance of power between state and federal courts. In the *Merrill Dow Pharmaceuticals Inc. v. Thompson* case, 478 U.S. 804 (1986), the Court held Congress's failure to provide a federal cause of action for violation of federal warning label statutes indicated congressional intent to bar federal jurisdiction over such claims. *Merrill Dow* involved state tort claims that would inundate the federal courts if the Court granted jurisdiction. In this case, however, due to the nature of the claim, there is no fear of distorting the division of labor between state and federal courts. That factor, coupled with the federal government's strong interest in the collection of taxes, provide a sound basis for federal question jurisdiction. Affirmed.

▶ ANALYSIS

Grable was a unanimous decision. Those who objected to the granting of federal jurisdiction feared it would open the flood gates to any state law claims that tangentially involved a federal interest, despite the lack of a federal cause of action. As the Supreme Court noted, the limiting factor is the type of case involved. Since this decision, there has not been any measureable increase in cases filed alleging "federal interest" jurisdiction.

■═■

Quicknotes

FEDERAL QUESTION JURISDICTION The authority of the federal courts to hear and determine in the first instance matters pertaining to the federal Constitution, federal law, or treaties of the United States.

REMOVAL Petition by a defendant to move the case to another court.

■═■

Erie R.R. Co. v. Tompkins

Railroad (D) v. Injured pedestrian (P)

304 U.S. 64 (1938).

NATURE OF CASE: Action to recover damages for personal injury allegedly caused by negligent conduct.

FACT SUMMARY: In a personal injury suit, federal district court trial judge refused to apply applicable state law because such law was "general" (judge-made) and not embodied in any statute.

RULE OF LAW
Although the 1789 Rules of Decision Act left federal courts unfettered to apply their own rules of procedure in common-law actions brought in federal court, state law governs substantive issues. State law includes not only statutory law, but case law as well.

FACTS: Tompkins (P) was walking in a right of way parallel to some railroad tracks when an Erie Railroad (D) train came by. Tompkins (P) was struck and injured by what he would, at trial, claim to be an open door extending from one of the rail cars. Under Pennsylvania case law (the applicable law since the accident occurred there), state courts would have treated Tompkins (P) as a trespasser in denying him recovery for other than wanton or willful misconduct on Erie's (D) part. Under "general" law, recognized in federal courts, Tompkins (P) would have been regarded as a licensee and would only have been obligated to show ordinary negligence. Because Erie (D) was a New York corporation, Tompkins (P) brought suit in a federal district court in New York, where he won a judgment for $30,000. Upon appeal to a Federal Circuit Court, the decision was affirmed.

ISSUE: Was the trial court in error in refusing to recognize state case law as the proper rule of decision in deciding the substantive issue of liability?

HOLDING AND DECISION: (Brandeis, J.) Yes. The Court's opinion is in four parts: (1) *Swift v. Tyson*, 41 U.S. (16 Pet.) 1 (1842), which held that federal courts exercising jurisdiction on the ground of diversity of citizenship need not, in matters of general jurisprudence, apply the unwritten law of the state as declared by its highest court, is overruled. Section 34 of the Federal Judiciary Act of 1789, c. 20, 28 U.S. § 725 requires that federal courts in all matters except those where some federal law is controlling, apply as their rules of decision the law of the state, unwritten as well as written. Up to this time, federal courts had assumed the power to make "general law" decisions even though Congress was powerless to enact "general law" statutes. (2) *Swift* had numerous political and social defects. The hoped-for uniformity among state courts had not occurred; there was no satisfactory way to distinguish between local and general law. On the other hand, *Swift* introduced grave discrimination by non-citizens against citizens. The privilege of selecting the court for resolving disputes rested with the non-citizen who could pick the more favorable forum. The resulting far-reaching discrimination was due to the broad province accorded "general law" in which many matters of seemingly local concern were included. Furthermore, local citizens could move out of the state and bring suit in a federal court if they were disposed to do so; corporations, similarly, could simply reincorporate in another state. More than statutory relief is involved here; the unconstitutionality of *Swift* is clear. (3) Except in matters governed by the Federal Constitution or by acts of Congress, the law to be applied in any case is the law of the state. There is no federal common law. The federal courts have no power derived from the Constitution or by Congress to declare substantive rules of common law applicable in a state whether they be "local" or "general" in nature. (4) The federal district court was bound to follow the Pennsylvania case law which would have denied recovery to Tompkins (P). Reversed.

CONCURRENCE IN PART: (Reed, J.) It is unnecessary to go beyond interpreting the meaning of "laws" in the Rules of Decision Act. Article III, and the Necessary and Proper Clause of Article I, of the Constitution might provide Congress with the power to declare rules of substantive law for federal courts to follow.

▶ ANALYSIS

Erie can fairly be characterized as the most significant and sweeping decision on civil procedure ever handed down by the U.S. Supreme Court. As interpreted in subsequent decisions, *Erie* held that while federal courts may apply their own rules of procedure, issues of substantive law must be decided in accord with the applicable state law usually the state in which the federal court sits. Note, however, how later Supreme Court decisions have made inroads into the broad doctrine enunciated here.

━■━■

Quicknotes

RULES OF DECISION ACT Provides that the laws of the several states shall be regarded as rules of decisions in civil action, except where the Constitution, treaties, or acts of Congress otherwise provide.

━■━■

Guaranty Trust Co. of New York v. York

Bank (D) v. Class alleging breach of trust (P)

326 U.S. 99 (1945).

NATURE OF CASE: Class action suit for breach of trust.

FACT SUMMARY: York (P) brought a class action suit against Guaranty Trust Co. (D) in federal court on diversity jurisdiction. The action was barred in the state courts by the statute of limitations and summary judgment was granted to Guaranty Trust (D) on that basis.

🏛 RULE OF LAW
In all cases where a federal court is exercising diversity jurisdiction, the outcome of the case should be substantially the same, so far as legal rules determine outcome, as it would be if tried in state court.

FACTS: York (P) brought suit in federal district court in New York on behalf of a class of persons allegedly damaged by Guaranty Trust Co.'s (D) breach of trust. The suit was brought in 1942, but complained of transactions occurring in 1931. Guaranty Trust (D) was granted a summary judgment on the grounds that the action was barred by the New York statute of limitations and that this suit being heard on diversity jurisdiction was governed by the statute. The court of appeals reversed, stating that suits in equity were not controlled by the state statute of limitations.

ISSUE: Where a suit brought in federal court on diversity jurisdiction would be barred by statute if brought in the state court, may the federal court nonetheless hear the case on its merits?

HOLDING AND DECISION: (Frankfurter, J.) No. Since this Court's decision in *Erie v. Tompkins*, 304 U.S. 64 (1938), a considerable amount of divergence has developed over what matters are procedural and what are substantive. Since these two concepts are fluid and situation controlled in most instances, the debate misses the underlying rationale of *Erie*. When sitting in diversity jurisdiction, a federal court is but another state court. The controlling factor is whether, by reason of application of differing federal rules, an outcome substantially different would result than if the case were brought in state court. The rules of law applied to the case cannot allow or bar recovery in the federal court where an opposite result would occur in the state court. For that reason, the summary judgment granted by the trial court is sustained. Reversed and remanded.

▶ ANALYSIS

The outcome determinative test enunciated in this case developed to the point where many observers and members of the judiciary felt that the federal courts had become unnecessarily slavish to the states. The cases developed to a point where, in one instance, a corporation qualified to sue by federal law was barred from bringing suit in a diversity action since it would not be qualified to bring suit in the state court. As was inevitable, the pendulum began to swing back as illustrated by the next two cases, particularly *Hanna v. Plumber*, in which the federal courts reasserted their independence.

Quicknotes

CLASS ACTION A suit commenced by a representative on behalf of an ascertainable group that is too large to appear in court, who shares a commonality of interests and who will benefit from a successful result.

DIVERSITY JURISDICTION The authority of a federal court to hear and determine cases involving $10,000 or more and in which the parties are citizens of different states, or in which one party is an alien.

STATUTE OF LIMITATIONS A law prescribing the period in which a legal action may be commenced.

SUMMARY JUDGMENT Judgment rendered by a court in response to a motion by one of the parties, claiming that the lack of a question of material fact in respect to an issue warrants disposition of the issue without consideration by the jury.

Byrd v. Blue Ridge Rural Elec. Coop., Inc.

Injured employee (P) v. General contractor (D)

356 U.S. 525 (1958).

NATURE OF CASE: Appeal by defendant in a workman's compensation suit.

FACT SUMMARY: An injured employee of subcontractor sued the prime contractor in federal court on diversity jurisdiction. The prime contractor asserted a defense which it claimed was to be ruled on by the judge, not a jury, according to controlling state law. A jury decided against the contractor on the defense asserted.

RULE OF LAW
A federal court sitting in diversity jurisdiction is obligated to enforce the substantive law of the state in which it sits unless there is a compelling federal policy to the contrary.

FACTS: Byrd (P) was an employee of a subcontractor to Blue Ridge Rural Electric Coop., Inc. (Blue Ridge) (D) and was injured on the job in South Carolina. South Carolina provided a workman's compensation system for statutorily defined employees. Byrd (P) sued Blue Ridge (D) in federal district court in South Carolina on the grounds of diversity jurisdiction. Blue Ridge (D) asserted a defense that, as Byrd (P) was a statutory employee of the subcontractor, his exclusive remedy was in workman's compensation. Blue Ridge (D) further contended that the issue of whether Byrd was a statutory employee was to be decided by the judge, not a jury, since the Supreme Court of South Carolina had held that this issue of fact was for the judge to decide and not a jury. The trial court submitted the factual determination of the defense to a jury which found in favor of Byrd (P). Blue Ridge (D) appealed.

ISSUE: Must a federal court sitting in diversity jurisdiction give force to a substantive law or policy of the state where there exists an express federal policy to the contrary?

HOLDING AND DECISION: (Brennan, J.) No. In *Erie v. Tompkins*, 304 U.S. 64 (1938), it was held that a federal court sitting in diversity jurisdiction must decide the issues presented on the basis of prevailing law of the state where the federal court sat. This doctrine was intended to embrace the substantive law of the forum state. The Erie Doctrine has been expanded to include procedural law where the outcome of the decision would be affected by employment of federal procedure. However, in this case, the state court decision relied on appears to be a rule based on habit or custom rather than substantive policy of the state. Further, there are countervailing considerations of strong federal policy. The Seventh Amendment to the Constitution is strong policy in favor of jury determination of issues of fact. There is no indication that jury determination of the factual issues of the Blue Ridge (D) defense would

produce an outcome different than if a determination were rendered by a judge. In view of the lack of showing compelling state policy and the existence of strong federal policy, the trial was correct in submitting the issue to a jury. Reversed and remanded.

CONCURRENCE AND DISSENT: (Whittaker, J.) The federal district court is bound to apply the law of the state in which it sits so that the state court "across the street" would not reach a different conclusion than that reached by the federal court. As South Carolina law requires the court, not the jury, to determine whether jurisdiction over the subject matter of cases like the one here is vested in its industrial commission, it would seem that the jurisdictional issue should have been determined here by the judge, not the jury.

ANALYSIS

The pendulum has begun to swing back. Prior to *Erie v. Tompkins* the federal courts were thought to be independent of state law either substantive or procedural. After *Erie v. Tompkins*, the federal courts became almost fanatically slavish to state law. Then, as this case illustrates, the federal courts began to reassert their independence. The countervailing considerations doctrine involving federal policy was invoked to allow a federal court to disregard almost all state procedural law and, in some cases, even substantive law. While initially, the countervailing considerations were found to be in the federal Constitution, soon the base would be broadened to include federal statutes as well.

Quicknotes

DIVERSITY JURISDICTION The authority of a federal court to hear and determine cases involving $10,000 or more and in which the parties are citizens of different states, or in which one party is an alien.

ERIE DOCTRINE Federal courts must apply state substantive law and federal procedural law.

Hanna v. Plumer

Ohio resident (P) v. Executor of Mass. decedent (D)

380 U.S. 460 (1965).

NATURE OF CASE: Appeal from an action for personal injuries.

FACT SUMMARY: Hanna (P), who brought suit in federal district court in Massachusetts, served Plumer (D) according to federal rules rather than state rules, which the trial court held to be a violation of the Erie Doctrine.

🏛 RULE OF LAW
Where a question arises under a federal rule of procedure, the rule should be applied unless it is shown that the Supreme Court and Congress erred in their prima facie judgment that the rule in question transgresses either the Rules Enabling Act or constitutional restrictions.

FACTS: Hanna (P), an Ohio resident, brought suit against the executor of a deceased Massachusetts resident in Massachusetts federal district court. According to Federal Rule of Civil Procedure 4(d)(1), Plumer (D) was served by having copies of the complaint left at his house with "someone of suitable age and discretion residing therein." Under Massachusetts law, in-hand service of process was required. Plumer (D) moved to dismiss the action on grounds that under the Erie Doctrine, the rules as to service were substantive, not procedural, and thus state rules should have been followed. The district court dismissed, the court of appeals affirmed, and Hanna (P) appealed.

ISSUE: Where a question arises under a Federal Rule of Procedure, should the Rule be applied?

HOLDING AND DECISION: (Warren, C.J.) Yes. Where a question arises under a Federal Rule of Procedure, the Rule should be applied unless it is shown that the Supreme Court and Congress erred in their prima facie judgment that the Rule in question transgresses either the Rules Enabling Act or constitutional restrictions. Under the Rules Enabling Act, the Supreme Court determines the rules of civil practice and procedure in federal courts. And while these rules cannot but help affect rights of the litigants, they cannot affect substantive rights. Here, application of state law would not have barred recovery, but only modify how the litigation would begin. That would not seem to affect a substantial right. Furthermore, *Erie* has never been used to void a federal rule. Only where a federal rule has not been as broad as the losing party argued, has substantive state law been used to fill the gap. The court, in making or formulating rules must measure those rules against the Rules Enabling Act and the Constitution, but it need not wholly blind itself to the degree to which the rule makes the

character and result of the federal litigation stray from the course it would follow in state courts. Reversed.

CONCURRENCE: (Harlan, J.) To determine if a rule is substantive or procedural, the court should inquire as to whether the choice would substantially affect those primary decisions respecting human conduct which our constitutional system leaves to state regulation.

▶ ANALYSIS

In *Sabich v. Wilson*, 312 U.S. 1, 14 (1941), the Court said, "The test must be whether a rule really regulates procedure the judicial process for enforcing rights and duties recognized by substantive law and for justly administering remedy and redress for disregard or infraction of them." This has been criticized as ignoring the statutory requirement that the rules not infringe substantive rights. It is possible that Congress's failure to strike down the rules during their "grace period" gives them statutory validity.

■═■

Quicknotes

ENABLING ACT A statute that confers new powers upon a person or entity.

ERIE DOCTRINE Federal courts must apply state substantive law and federal procedural law.

FEDERAL RULE OF CIVIL PROCEDURE 4(d)(1) Governs service of process.

■═■

Walker v. Armco Steel Corp.

Injured worker (P) v. Manufacturer (D)

446 U.S. 740 (1980).

NATURE OF CASE: Review of dismissal of personal injury action.

FACT SUMMARY: Walker (P) contended that, in a diversity action, Federal Rule of Civil Procedure 3 prevailed over a state law governing when, for statute of limitation purposes, an action is commenced.

RULE OF LAW
In a diversity action, state law regarding when an action is commenced prevails over Federal Rule of Civil Procedure 3.

FACTS: Walker (P) filed a personal injury action in federal district court in Oklahoma against Armco Steel Corp. (D), jurisdiction being based on diversity. The complaint had been filed less than two years after the cause of action arose but was served well after this period elapsed. Under the Oklahoma statute of limitations, an action was not considered "commenced" against a defendant until service was effected. The district court rejected Walker's (P) argument that Federal Rule of Civil Procedure 3, which provided that commencement of an action occurred upon filing, was applicable and dismissed the action under Oklahoma's two-year statute of limitations. The Tenth Circuit affirmed, and the Supreme Court granted review.

ISSUE: In a diversity action, does state law regarding when an action is commenced prevail over Federal Rule of Civil Procedure 3?

HOLDING AND DECISION: (Marshall, J.) Yes. In a diversity action, state law regarding when an action is commenced prevails over Federal Rule of Civil Procedure 3. This Court long ago held that the statute of limitations in an action is a matter of substantive law, which federal courts are bound to follow in a diversity case. Anything which would tend to toll or extend the statute must be considered likewise a matter of substantive law, and state law must prevail in such a situation. This would seem to decide the issue here. However, Walker (P) contended that, when a provision of the Federal Rules of Civil Procedure conflicts with a state rule, the federal rule must apply. This is true, but only when the scope of the federal rule is broad enough to truly conflict with state rules. There is no indication that Federal Rule of Civil Procedure 3 was intended to deal with the statute of limitations; rather, it merely sets the point from which the various timing requirements of the Federal Rules of Civil Procedure begin to run. As no conflict between Oklahoma's rule and the Federal Rules exists, the Oklahoma rule prevails. Affirmed.

ANALYSIS

Conflicts law often involves not so much the resolution of a conflict as recognition thereof. Generally speaking, when a state rule conflicts with a federal rule in a diversity action, the federal rule prevails. As the present case demonstrates, the trick is often recognizing whether a conflict in fact exists. Here it did not.

Quicknotes

DIVERSITY JURISDICTION The authority of a federal court to hear and determine cases involving $75,000 or more and in which the parties are citizens of different states, or in which one party is an alien.

STATUTE OF LIMITATIONS A law prescribing the period in which a legal action may be commenced.

Gasperini v. Center for Humanities, Inc.

Injured owner (P) v. Borrower (D)

518 U.S. 415 (1996)

NATURE OF CASE: Review of judgment setting aside award of damages for breach of contract, conversion, and negligence.

FACT SUMMARY: A federal circuit court, hearing a case on diversity jurisdiction, let stand a jury verdict of $450,000 for lost photographic slides; the court of appeals, applying New York law governing excessive damage awards, set aside the verdict.

🏛 RULE OF LAW
A state law governing the excessiveness or inadequacy of compensation awards does not violate the Seventh Amendment's prohibition against re-examination of a fact tried by a jury so long as the state standard is applied by the federal trial court judge and appellate control of the trial court ruling is limited to review for abuse of discretion.

FACTS: Gasperini (P), a journalist, agreed to supply his original color transparencies to The Center for Humanities, Inc. (D), for use in an educational videotape. He selected 300 slides, and the Center (D) used 110 of them in the video. The Center (D) agreed to return the slides, but it could not find them at the end of the project. Gasperini (P) filed suit in the U.S. District Court for the Southern District of New York, invoking the court's diversity jurisdiction. He alleged several state law claims. The Center (D) conceded liability, and the issue of damages was tried before a jury. The jury awarded Gasperini (P) $450,000 in compensatory damages, $1,500 for each of the 300 slides. The Center (D) filed a motion for a new trial, attacking the verdict on excessiveness grounds. The district court denied the motion. The court of appeals, however, vacated the jury's verdict. Applying New York's CPLR § 5501(c), which permits the ordering of a new trial when an award deviates materially from "reasonable compensation," the court concluded that evidence at trial was insufficient to support the $450,000 damage award. The appellate court ordered a new trial unless Gasperini (P) accepted an award of $100,000. Gasperini (P) appealed to the Supreme Court.

ISSUE: Does a state law governing the excessiveness or inadequacy of compensation awards violate the Seventh Amendment's prohibition against re-examining a fact tried by a jury?

HOLDING AND DECISION: (Ginsburg, J.) No. A state law governing the excessiveness or inadequacy of compensation awards does not violate the Seventh Amendment's prohibition against re-examination of a fact tried by a jury so long as the state standard is applied by the federal trial court judge and appellate control of the trial court

ruling is limited to review for abuse of discretion. The Seventh Amendment, which governs proceedings in federal court, but not in state court, provides that "no fact tried by a jury shall be otherwise re-examined in any Court of the United States, than according to the rules of the common law." When a federal court hears a case under diversity jurisdiction, the court applies state substantive law and federal procedural law. The "deviates materially" standard of CPLR § 5501(c) contains a procedural instruction, but it is substantive law insofar as it is outcome effective. Thus, the district court has the responsibility to apply state laws governing excessive damage awards, and the appellate court must review for abuse of discretion. In this case, the district court should have applied § 5501(c) to determine whether the award deviated materially from reasonableness. The appellate court was constrained to review for abuse of discretion only. The judgment of the appellate court is vacated, and that court is instructed to remand so that the trial judge may test the jury's verdict against CPLR § 5501(c)'s "deviates materially" standard.

DISSENT: (Stevens, J.) The Seventh Amendment in no way limits the power of a federal appellate court sitting in diversity to decide whether a jury's award of damages exceeds a limit established by state law.

DISSENT: (Scalia, J.) The majority believes that allowing the district court to review jury verdicts under the "deviates materially" standard will give effect to state purposes without disrupting the federal system. However, changing the standard by which trial judges review jury verdicts does disrupt the federal system.

▶ ANALYSIS

The seminal case, *Erie R. Co. v. Tompkins*, 304 U.S. 64 (1938), first specified the "substantive" versus "procedural" distinction mentioned in this case. The goal of *Erie* was to prevent forum-shopping between state and federal court. However, Justice Scalia argued that by adopting different standards of appellate review between state and federal courts, the incentive to forum-shop was enhanced. Just how influential a deviation in appellate review standards will be when parties are selecting the forum to litigate claims remains to be seen.

━▣▮

Quicknotes

DIVERSITY JURISDICTION The authority of a federal court to hear and determine cases involving $75,000 or more

Continued on next page.

and in which the parties are citizens of different states, or in which one party is an alien.

ERIE DOCTRINE Federal courts must apply state substantive law and federal procedural law.

SEVENTH AMENDMENT Provides that no fact tried by a jury shall be otherwise re-examined in any court of the United States, other than according to the rules of the common law.

Semtek International Inc. v. Lockheed Martin Corp.

California company (P) v. Maryland company (D)

531 U.S. 497 (2001).

NATURE OF CASE: Review of dismissal of a state breach of contract action due to the res judicata effect of a federal diversity judgment.

FACT SUMMARY: After a federal district court dismissed a breach of contract complaint under California's two-year statute of limitations, Semtek International Inc. (P) filed the same action in Maryland, which has a longer statute of limitations, but the court dismissed the case on res judicata grounds.

> **RULE OF LAW**
> Where there is no conflict with federal interests, the claim preclusive effect of a dismissal by a federal court sitting in diversity should be determined according to the law of the state in which the federal court is sitting.

FACTS: Semtek International Inc. (P) sued Lockheed Martin Corp. (D) for breach of contract in California state court and Lockheed (D) removed the case to federal court. After the court dismissed the action with prejudice because the statute of limitations had run, Semtek (P) filed the same complaint in Maryland, where Lockheed was a citizen and the statute of limitations was longer. The Maryland trial court granted Lockheed's (D) motion to dismiss for res judicata and Semtek (P) appealed, arguing that a California state court would not have accorded claim preclusive effect to a statute of limitations dismissal by one of its own courts. The Maryland appeals court affirmed the dismissal, holding that the res judicata effect of a federal diversity judgment was a matter of federal law and that the judgment was preclusive. The Supreme Court granted certiorari.

ISSUE: Where there is no conflict with federal interests, should the claim preclusive effect of a dismissal by a federal court sitting in diversity be determined according to the law of the state in which the federal court is sitting?

HOLDING AND DECISION: (Scalia, J.) Yes. Where there is no conflict with federal interests, the claim preclusive effect of a dismissal by a federal court sitting in diversity should be determined according to the law of the state in which the federal court is sitting. The claim preclusive effect, in Maryland, of the California diversity judgment should not be based on either the precedent in *Dupasseur v. Rochereau,* 21 Wall. 130, 135 (1875), a case decided under the Conformity Act of 1872, which required federal courts to apply the procedural law of the forum state, or on Federal Rule of Civil Procedure 14(b). Despite the repeal of the Conformity Act and the promulgation of the Erie Doctrine, the result decreed by *Dupasseur* continues to be correct for

diversity cases. Since state law is at issue, there is no need for a uniform federal rule. The law that should be applied is that law that would be applied by state courts in the state in which the federal diversity court sits. Reversed and remanded.

> ▶ **ANALYSIS**
>
> Since California would not have accorded claim preclusive effect, it was error for the Maryland court to do so. Under *Erie,* federal courts are to apply the substantive state law of the state in which they sit. When the application of state law would influence the outcome of the case, state law should be applied.

■═■

Quicknotes

CERTIORARI A discretionary writ issued by a superior court to an inferior court in order to review the lower court's decisions; the Supreme Court's writ ordering such review.

DIVERSITY JURISDICTION The authority of a federal court to hear and determine cases involving $75,000 or more and in which the parties are citizens of different states, or in which one party is an alien.

ERIE DOCTRINE Federal courts must apply state substantive law and federal procedural law.

RES JUDICATA The rule of law that a final judgment by a court precludes subsequent litigation between the parties regarding the same cause of action.

■═■

Klaxon Co. v. Stentor Elec. Mfg. Co.

Delaware corporation (D) v. New York corporation (P)

313 U.S. 487 (1941).

NATURE OF CASE: Damages for breach of contract.

FACT SUMMARY: Stentor Elec. Mfg. Co. (P) received judgment for breach of contract based on Klaxon's (D) failure to manufacture and sell certain goods. Klaxon Co. (D) appeals that part of the order allowing interest on the damages from when the suit was filed.

RULE OF LAW

Federal district courts must apply the conflict of law rules of the states in which they sit when deciding a case based upon diversity jurisdiction.

FACTS: In 1918, Stentor Elec. Mfg. Co. (P) transferred its entire business to Klaxon Co. (D) in return for a contractual promise by Klaxon (D) to use best efforts to promote the sale of certain items upon which Stentor (P) retained patent rights. Stentor (P) was a New York corporation, Klaxon (D) a Delaware corporation, and the agreement was executed and partially performed in New York. In 1929, Stentor (P), suing in diversity jurisdiction, sued Klaxon (D) in federal district court in Delaware for breach of the agreement. A judgment of $100,000 was rendered in Stentor's (P) favor. Stentor then moved to modify the judgment to add interest at the rate of six percent from the date the action was commenced. The motion was based on a New York statute and was granted by the district court on the grounds that the issue was substantive and that New York law governed the dispute. Klaxon (D) appealed the motion, asserting that the district court was bound to follow the substantive law of Delaware in diversity actions. The circuit court of appeals affirmed on the basis that the New York rule was the "better view."

ISSUE: In a diversity jurisdiction case, must the federal courts apply the conflict of law rules prevailing in the states in which the court sits?

HOLDING AND DECISION: (Reed, J.) Yes. Federal courts cannot make independent determinations of what the law in the state in which they sit should be, but must apply the conflicts rules of the states when deciding diversity jurisdiction cases. There is no independent general law of conflicts. Each state in the federal system is free to determine whether a given matter is to be governed by the law of the forum or some other law. Therefore, there must be uniformity within each state so as to avoid forum shopping between federal and state courts within each state. The proper function of the federal courts is to determine what the state law is, and not what the law should be. Any other decision would lead to a disruption of the equal administration of justice in state and federal courts which sit in the same state and apply the same state law. Reversed and remanded.

▶ ANALYSIS

The *Klaxon* case amplifies the *Erie* rule to include the state conflict of law rules where they apply to outcome determinative issues. On remand, the circuit court found that the Delaware conflicts rules referred the issue to New York law, and thus the decision remained the same through the use of differing rules.

Quicknotes

DIVERSITY JURISDICTION The authority of a federal court to hear and determine cases involving $75,000 or more and in which the parties are citizens of different states, or in which one party is an alien.

FORUM-SHOPPING Refers to a situation in which one party to an action seeks to have the matter heard and determined by a court, or in a jurisdiction, that will provide it with the most favorable result.

Clearfield Trust Co. v. United States

Bank (D) v. Federal government (P)

318 U.S. 363 (1943).

NATURE OF CASE: Appeal from reversal of a holding that the action was barred by unreasonable delay.

FACT SUMMARY: The Government (P) sought reimbursement on a check it issued to one Barner, who never received it, but was endorsed through forgery and honored by Clearfield Trust Co. (D).

🏛 **RULE OF LAW**
The rights and duties of the United States on commercial paper which it issues are governed by federal rather than local law.

FACTS: On April 28, 1936, the Government (P) issued a check for $24.20 to Barner for services rendered to the Works Progress Administration. Unexplainably, Barner never received the check. The check apparently was stolen and the endorsement forged and the check was transferred to J.C. Penney Co. in exchange for cash and merchandise. J.C. Penney endorsed the check over to Clearfield Trust Co. (D) and Clearfield (D) endorsed the check over to the Federal Reserve Bank of Philadelphia. Clearfield (D) guaranteed prior endorsements as required by Treasury regulations. Neither Clearfield (D) nor Penney know of or suspected a forgery. On May 10, 1936, Barner informed his foreman that he never received his check. Clearfield (D) and Penney did not learn of the forgery until January 12, 1937. Clearfield (D) was first notified that the Government (P) was seeking reimbursement on August 31, 1937. The Government's (P) cause of action was based upon the guarantee of the endorsement and was brought in federal district court in Pennsylvania. That court held that Pennsylvania law applied under the Erie Doctrine, and since the Government (P) unreasonably delayed in giving notice of forgery, the action was barred. The court of appeals reversed, and Clearfield (D) appealed.

ISSUE: Are the rights and duties of the United States on commercial paper which it issues governed by federal rather than local law?

HOLDING AND DECISION: (Douglas, J.) Yes. The rights and duties of the United States on commercial paper which it issues are governed by federal rather than local law. When the Government (P) disburses its funds or pays its debts, it exercises a constitutional power. Here, the authority to issue the check was derived from the Constitution and was in no way dependent on the laws of Pennsylvania or any other state. The Government (P) issues commercial paper on such a vast scale and in all states so that the application of state law would subject the rights and duties of the Government (P) to great uncertainty. Thus, the Government (P) was not barred from bringing suit because Clearfield (D) had not shown that the delay in receiving notice had caused it injury. Affirmed.

▶ **ANALYSIS**

This case demonstrates that the court has failed to be explicit on the question of what is its authority for creation of federal common law. Some lower courts have indicated that in cases where the United States is a party, such as cases in admiralty and suits between states, the federal courts have lawmaking powers. Note, however, that the Erie Doctrine is not limited to diversity cases; only in cases where the court may effect a policy derived from the Constitution or from a valid act of Congress may the federal courts make substantive law.

■▬■

Quicknotes

ERIE DOCTRINE Federal courts must apply state substantive law and federal procedural law.

■▬■

Bank of America v. Parnell

Bondholder (P) v. Payee (D)

352 U.S. 29 (1956).

NATURE OF CASE: Action to recover proceeds from wrongfully converted bonds.

FACT SUMMARY: Parnell (D) and others converted 73 corporate bonds stolen from Bank of America (P).

RULE OF LAW
Federal courts must apply federal common law (as created to effect statutory patterns enacted by Congress) to determine the immediate interests of the federal government where it is involved in a transaction, but where the transaction involved is essentially a private one between private parties, local law must govern.

FACTS: In 1944, 73 Home Owners' Loan Corporation bonds, belonging to Bank of America (P) and insured by the federal government (making them government commercial paper) disappeared while being prepared for presentation for payment. Though they were originally to mature in 1952, they were called in 1944. In 1948, they showed up at the First National Bank in Indiana (D) where Parnell (D) presented them for payment. First National (D) forwarded them to the Federal Reserve Bank of Cleveland (D) which cashed them and permitted First National (D) to pay Parnell (D). Bank of America (P) sued all to recover the value of the bonds. At trial, the issue of burden of proof was raised. Under appropriate state law, the burden of proof shifts to Parnell (D) and the banks (to establish that they acquired the bonds "innocently, honestly, and in good faith") after Bank of America (P) establishes that the bonds were stolen. Using this standard, the trial court jury brought in verdicts against all defendants. The court of appeals, however, reversed on the grounds that, because commercial paper was involved, the proper standard for burden of proof should be federal common law, since commercial paper necessarily involves the interests of the federal government as a party. Under federal common law, the burden is upon Bank of America to show that Parnell (D), et al., acted in bad faith. Since, under federal law, the bonds were not "overdue" at the time of presentation (whereas they would be under state law), Parnell (D), et al., could not be found in bad faith since they would be under no notice that they could not be properly cashed. As such, the court of appeals ordered the trial court to direct a verdict for all defendants. Bank of America (P) appealed.

ISSUE: Does the mere involvement of federally insured commercial paper in a transaction necessarily require the application of federal common law by a federal court?

HOLDING AND DECISION: (Frankfurter, J.) No. Federal courts must apply federal common law (as created by courts to effect statutory patterns enacted by Congress) to determine the immediate interests of the federal government where it is involved in a transaction, but where the transaction involved is essentially a private one between private parties, local law must govern. In *Clearfield Trust Co. v. U.S.*, 318 U.S. 363 (1943), it was held that the danger of uncertainty of federal government rights in that case required that federal common law be applied to define those rights. In that case, a stolen government payroll check was involved, and federal government rights necessarily were involved as well. Here, however, federal rights are involved only to the extent of the government's insurable interest in them. Since the transaction here (i.e., the conversion) does not in any way alter this interest, it should be determined by local state law as any diversity suit between private parties. Judgment reversed and case remanded.

DISSENT: (Black, J.) There should be a per se standard for all commercial paper cases; and courts should treat all such cases as federal common law cases.

ANALYSIS

This case points up the federal common-law theory of federal questions. In short, it states that cases which involve federal court interpretations of federal government rights (i.e., common law) are federal questions for which the Supremacy Clause requires federal law be applied. The making of federal common law (i.e., case law to effect the implementation of congressional statutes, treaties, etc.) is viewed as an implied power of the courts, necessarily mandated by the very existence of the federal court system.

Quicknotes

COMMERCIAL PAPER A negotiable instrument; a written promise, signed by the promisee, to pay a specified sum of money to the promisor either on demand or on a specified date.

CONVERSION The act of depriving an owner of his property without permission or justification.

SUPREMACY CLAUSE Art. VI, Sec. 2, of the Constitution, which provides that federal action must prevail over inconsistent state action.

Banco Nacional de Cuba v. Sabbatino

Bank (P) v. Receiver (D)

376 U.S. 398 (1964).

NATURE OF CASE: Action to recover payments owed.

FACT SUMMARY: The Cuban government sought to recover money owed pursuant to a contract for the sale of sugar.

🏛 RULE OF LAW
The scope of the act-of-state doctrine must be determined according to federal law.

FACTS: In response to a U.S. reduction of Cuba's quota for sugar imports, Cuba nationalized the property of Americans in Cuba, including that belonging to Compania Azucarera Vertientes (CAV), a sugar corporation largely owned by U.S. residents. CAV had contracted to sell the sugar to Farr, Whitlock & Co., a U.S. commodities broker. Farr entered into a second contract to buy sugar from the Cuban government. Farr shipped the sugar and received payment but turned the proceeds over to CAV's receiver, Sabbatino (D). Cuba assigned its rights under the contract to Banco Nacional (P), which filed suit. The district court found in favor of Sabbatino (D) and the court of appeals affirmed.

ISSUE: Must the scope of the act-of-state doctrine be determined according to federal law?

HOLDING AND DECISION: (Harlan, J.) Yes. The scope of the act-of-state doctrine must be determined according to federal law. [The Court first held that the application of the act-of-state doctrine was neither compelled by international law nor by the Constitution.] The act-of-state doctrine expresses the judicial determination that courts should not pass on the validity of acts of other sovereign states. It is a federal issue, however. If the state courts were left free to formulate their own rules for such cases, the purpose of the act-of-state doctrine would be eviscerated. Issues of international law are federal issues and should not be left to parochial state interpretations. [Because a challenge to the Cuban government's decree would interfere with negotiations being carried out by the Executive Branch, the decree could not be challenged. The act-of-state doctrine is also discussed in the brief for *Banco Nacional de Cuba v Sabbatino* in Chapter 8.]

▶ ANALYSIS

Relying on *Hinderlider v. La Plata River Ditch Co.*, 304 U.S. 92, the Court equates the federal interest in the act-of-state doctrine to that of equitably apportioning interstate waters, and cautions against the dangers of applying the Erie doctrine to legal problems affecting international relations.

■=■

Quicknotes

ACT-OF-STATE DOCTRINE Prohibits United States courts from investigating acts of other countries committed within the borders of the other country.

■=■

English v. General Electric Co.

Whistleblower (P) v. Nuclear plant employer (D)

496 U.S. 72 (1990).

NATURE OF CASE: Appeal of dismissal on grounds of federal preemption.

FACT SUMMARY: Vera English (P), a laboratory technician at a nuclear plant managed by General Electric Company (GE) (D), complained to management and to the federal government about safety violations at the plant. After she deliberately failed to clean a work area contaminated during an earlier shift with uranium, she was fired. She filed a retaliation claim, and the court dismissed the claim on the ground that federal law preempted it.

RULE OF LAW
Federal law does not preempt a state-law claim for intentional infliction of emotional distress by a nuclear power plant whistleblower.

FACTS: Vera English (P) was a laboratory technician at a nuclear plant managed by General Electric Company (GE) (D). She complained to GE's (D) management and to the federal government about the failure of her co-workers to clean up radioactive spills in the laboratory. In response to GE's (D) failure to deal with the issue, English (P) deliberately failed to clean a work area contaminated during an earlier shift with uranium. She outlined the contaminated areas with red tape to make the spills conspicuous. A few days later, she called her supervisor's attention to the fact that the areas still had not been cleaned. GE (D) stopped work for inspection and cleaning of the laboratory, and then charged English (P) with a knowing failure to clean up radioactive contamination. She was reassigned and eventually fired. She filed a complaint with the Labor Department, charging GE (D) with violation of § 210(a) of the Energy Reorganization Act of 1974, which makes it unlawful for a nuclear industry employer to retaliate against an employee for reporting safety violations. An administrative law judge found a § 210(a) violation, but the Labor Department dismissed the complaint as untimely. English (P) then filed a diversity action in district court, seeking compensatory and punitive damages from GE (D), raising, among other things, a state-law claim for intentional infliction of emotional distress. The court dismissed the claim on the ground that it conflicted with three aspects of § 210 and was therefore preempted. The court of appeals affirmed.

ISSUE: Does federal law preempt a state-law claim for intentional infliction of emotional distress by a nuclear power plant whistleblower?

HOLDING AND DECISION: (Blackmun, J.) No. Federal law does not preempt a state-law claim for intentional infliction of emotional distress by a nuclear power plant whistleblower. There are three different kinds of preemption: express preemption, field preemption, and implied conflict preemption. First, Congress has not explicitly preempted her state-law tort action by inserting specific preemptive language into any of its laws governing the nuclear industry. Second, there is no clear indication that Congress, by enacting § 210, intended to preempt all state tort laws that traditionally have been available to claimants alleging outrageous conduct at the hands of an employer. While § 210 bears some relation to the field of nuclear safety, its chief purpose was the protection of employees. For a state law to fall within the preempted zone, it must have some direct and substantial effect on the decisions made by those who build or operate nuclear facilities concerning radiological safety levels, and this claim's effect on the nuclear safety decisions made by those who build and run nuclear facilities is not sufficiently direct and substantial. Third, and finally, English's (P) claim does not conflict with particular aspects of § 210. Neither the text nor the legislative history of § 210(g) reflects a congressional desire to preclude all relief, including state remedies, for a whistleblower who deliberately commits a safety violation. Even if that were Congress's intent, the federal interest would be served by preempting recovery by violators of safety standards. Here, the administrative law judge found that English (P) did not deliberately commit a violation. In addition, unless there is some specific suggestion in the text or legislative history otherwise, the failure of § 210 to provide general authorization for the Labor Department to award punitive damages for § 210(a) violations does not imply a congressional intent to bar a state action that permits such an award. Moreover, the timeframes provided for processing § 210 claims do not reflect a congressional decision that, in order to encourage the reporting of safety violations and retaliatory behavior, no whistleblower should be able to recover under any other law after the time for filing under § 210 has expired. Since many retaliatory incidents are a response to safety complaints made to the federal government, the government is already aware of these safety violations even if employees do not invoke § 210's remedial provisions. And finally, the suggestion that employees will forgo their § 210 options and rely solely on state remedies is simply too speculative a basis on which to rest a preemption finding. Reversed and remanded.

ANALYSIS

Note that briefs of amici curiae urging reversal were filed for the attorney general of North Carolina, for the National

Continued on next page.

Conference of State Legislatures, and for the Plaintiff Employment Lawyers Association. Briefs of amici curiae urging affirmance were filed for the Nuclear Management and Resources Council, Inc.

■■■

Quicknotes

DIVERSITY ACTION An action commenced by a citizen of one state against a citizen of another state or against an alien, involving an amount in controversy set by statute, over which the federal court has jurisdiction.

PREEMPTION Doctrine holding that matters of national interest take precedence over matters of local interest; the federal law takes precedence over state law.

PUNITIVE DAMAGES Damages exceeding the actual injury suffered for the purposes of punishment of the defendant, deterrence of the wrongful behavior or comfort to the plaintiff.

■■■

Testa v. Katt

Car purchaser (P) v. Car dealer (D)

330 U.S. 386 (1947).

NATURE OF CASE: Appeal from reversal of an award of damages under the Emergency Price Control Act.

FACT SUMMARY: Testa (P) sought treble damages in Rhode Island state court for Katt's (D) violation of the Federal Emergency Price Control Act for selling him an auto for more than the ceiling price.

🏛 RULE OF LAW
A state court cannot refuse to enforce a right arising from federal law for reasons of conflict with state policy or "want of wisdom" on part of Congress.

FACTS: Under the Emergency Price Control Act, anyone who sold goods for more than the price ceiling on those goods was liable to the buyer for treble the overcharge plus attorney's fees. The federal act created a right of action not only in federal court, but in state court as well. Testa (P) purchased a car in 1944 from Katt (D), a dealer, for $1,100, $210 above the ceiling price. Testa (P) brought suit under the act in Providence, Rhode Island, in the State District Court. He was awarded the full amount of damages possible under the act. On appeal to the State Superior Court, damages were reduced to the amount of overcharge plus fees. The State Supreme Court reversed on grounds that the federal statute was penal, and that it need not enforce penal laws of a government foreign in the international sense. It held that as the United States was foreign in the "private international" sense, it need not enforce the federal act. Testa (P) appealed.

ISSUE: Can a state court refuse to enforce a right arising from federal law for reasons of conflict with state policy or "want of wisdom" on part of Congress?

HOLDING AND DECISION: (Black, J.) No. A state court cannot refuse to enforce a right arising from federal law for reasons of conflict with state policy or "want of wisdom" on part of Congress. The Supremacy Clause of the Constitution provides that the Constitution, federal laws, and treaties are the supreme law of the land, that the judges in every state are bound by that supreme law, any state law, Constitution, or policy to the contrary notwithstanding. "The obligation of states to enforce... federal laws is not lessened by reason of the form in which they are cast or the remedy which they provide." For a state to say that federal policy being in conflict with its own proscribes enforcement of the federal act is to ignore the policy espoused by Congress for all the people and all the states. Rhode Island's failure to enforce the federal act violated the Supremacy Clause and necessitates reversal. Reversed and remanded.

▶ ANALYSIS

A state court must entertain a cause of action created under federal law providing jurisdiction in state courts. States may not discriminate against rights which arise under federal laws. Despite the rule of this case, the question of where Congress obtained the power to require state courts to exercise jurisdiction is left unanswered. Some suggest the Necessary and Proper Clause as the source for such power while others have inferred it to come from Congress's power to establish inferior courts.

■═■

Quicknotes

NECESSARY AND PROPER CLAUSE, ACT I, § 8 OF THE CONSTITUTION Enables Congress to make all laws that may be "necessary and proper" to execute its other, enumerated powers.

■═■

Howlett v. Rose

High school student (P) v. School board (D)

496 U.S 356 (1990).

NATURE OF CASE: Appeal of dismissal for lack of jurisdiction.

FACT SUMMARY: A high school student whose car was searched on school property and who was subsequently suspended brought a federal claim against the school board in state court. The state would not have immunity if the case were brought in a federal forum. But the state courts of Florida interpreted that state's waiver of sovereign immunity as not applying to section 1983 claims.

RULE OF LAW
A state-law "sovereign immunity" defense is not available to a school board in a § 1983 action brought in a state court that otherwise has jurisdiction, when such defense would not be available if the action were brought in a federal forum.

FACTS: A high school student sued the school board after his car was searched on school premises and he was suspended from school. He sued under 42 U.S.C. § 1983, which creates a remedy for violations of federal rights committed by persons acting under color of state law. The student claimed that his car was searched in violation of the Fourth and Fourteenth Amendments, and he was suspended without due process. He sought damages and injunctive relief. The court dismissed the complaint against the board for lack of jurisdiction. The state would not have immunity if the case were brought in a federal forum. But the state courts of Florida interpreted that state's waiver of sovereign immunity as not applying to § 1983 claims.

ISSUE: Is a state-law "sovereign immunity" defense available to a school board in a § 1983 action brought in a state court that otherwise has jurisdiction, when such defense would not be available if the action were brought in a federal forum?

HOLDING AND DECISION: (Stevens, J.) No. A state-law "sovereign immunity" defense is not available to a school board in a § 1983 action brought in a state court that otherwise has jurisdiction, when such defense would not be available if the action were brought in a federal forum. Federal law is enforceable in state courts because the Constitution and laws passed pursuant to it are as much laws in the States as laws passed by the state legislature. The Supremacy Clause makes those laws the supreme "Law of the Land." That Clause requires state courts to enforce that law according to their ordinary procedures. The Florida court's refusal to entertain a category of § 1983 claims, when the court entertains similar state-law actions against state defendants, violates the Supremacy Clause. Reversed and remanded.

ANALYSIS

In this case, the Florida courts interpreted the state's waiver of sovereign immunity as not applying to § 1983 claims. Since other similar claims were not subject to the sovereign immunity defense, the Supreme Court mandated that § 1983 claims could not be precluded. But note that the court also said that "[t]he requirement that a state court of competent jurisdiction treat federal law as the law of the land does not necessarily include within it a requirement that the State create a court competent to hear [a] case in which the federal claim is presented." Thus, as long as a state applies a rule of subject matter jurisdiction neutrally and not in a discriminatory manner, the state can refuse to provide a court of competent jurisdiction to hear § 1983 claims.

Quicknotes

DUE PROCESS The constitutional mandate requiring the courts to protect and enforce individuals' rights and liberties consistent with prevailing principles of fairness and justice and prohibiting the federal and state governments from such activities that deprive its citizens of life, liberty, or property interest.

FOURTEENTH AMENDMENT Declares that no state shall make or enforce any law that shall abridge the privileges and immunities of citizens of the United States. No state shall deny to any person within its jurisdiction the equal protection of the laws.

FOURTH AMENDMENT Provides that persons be secure as to their person and private belongings against unreasonable searches and seizures.

IMMUNITY Exemption from a legal obligation.

INJUNCTIVE RELIEF A court order issued as a remedy, requiring a person to do, or prohibiting that person from doing, a specific act.

JURISDICTION The authority of a court to hear and declare judgment in respect to a particular matter.

SOVEREIGN IMMUNITY Immunity of government from suit without its consent.

SUPREMACY CLAUSE Art. VI of the U.S. Constitution, which provides that federal action must prevail over inconsistent state action.

Dice v. Akron, Canton & Youngstown R.R.

Railroad fireman (P) v. Railroad (D)

342 U.S. 359 (1952).

NATURE OF CASE: Appeal from denial of damages under the Federal Employers' Liability Act.

FACT SUMMARY: Dice (P), a railroad fireman who was injured when Akron's (D) train jumped the track, alleged that he was defrauded when Akron (D) told him that the receipts he signed for $924.63 were not a full release of Akron's (D) liability to him when in fact they were.

RULE OF LAW

The right to trial by jury, being a substantial part of the rights accorded under the Federal Employers' Liability Act, it cannot be denied by a state court as a mere local rule of procedure.

FACTS: Dice (P), a railroad fireman, suffered serious injury when the Akron (B) train in which he rode jumped the tracks. Dice (P) received $924.63 in payments from Akron (D) for which he signed receipts. Akron (D) represented that the receipts were nothing more than that, but actually they were a release of any liability on the part of Akron (D). Dice (P) brought an action under the Federal Employers' Liability Act in an Ohio trial court. He was awarded $25,000, but Akron (D) was given judgment in N.O.V. because of Dice's (P) "supine negligence" in failing to read the release. The judgment N.O.V. was reversed by the state court of appeals on grounds that federal law controlled and that the verdict of the jury must stand as there was ample evidence of fraud. The Ohio Supreme Court reversed that ruling on grounds that state, not federal law, controlled; that under that law, a man of ordinary intelligence who can read is bound by a release he signs; and under Ohio law, factual issues as to fraud were properly decided by the judge, not the jury. Dice (P) appealed.

ISSUE: Is the right to trial too substantial a part of the rights accorded under the Federal Employers' Liability Act to be denied by a state court as a mere rule of local procedure?

HOLDING AND DECISION: (Black, J.) Yes. The right to trial by jury being a substantial part of the rights accorded under the Federal Employers' Liability Act cannot be denied by a state court as a mere local rule of procedure. Validity of releases under the Act raises a federal question to be determined under federal, not state law. Second, Ohio's rule, in effect, says that an employee trusts his employer at his peril. This policy is contra to that of the Act and is against the modern trend. Third, Ohio gave Dice (P) the usual jury trial on issues of negligence, but allowed the judge to determine questions as to fraud. A state cannot provide a jury trial for cases arising under a federal act, but

single out a certain issue to be determined not by the jury, but by the judge. The right to a jury trial is a basic and fundamental feature of federal jurisprudence. Thus, it was error to say it was a mere local rule of procedure. Reversed and remanded.

DISSENT: (Frankfurter, J.) While it was correct to reverse, the grounds stated for reversal were in error. A state court is under no duty to treat the conduct of a trial arising under a federal law any differently than under state law. Rather, here, reversal was required for misapplication of the standard applied for validity of releases.

ANALYSIS

In the situation as presented in this case where a state court entertains an action based on federal law, the same considerations that determine the use of federal procedure in diversity cases appear to govern the applicability of state procedural laws. Federal questions have been held to include the burden of proof respecting contributory negligence and the sufficiency of the evidence to sustain a verdict. As it is, the majority of cases involving the Federal Employers' Liability Act have been concerned with sufficiency of the evidence. It seems clear that permitting state law to govern these issues would burden strong federal policies.

Quicknotes

CONTRIBUTORY NEGLIGENCE Behavior on the part of an injured plaintiff falling below the standard of ordinary care that contributes to the defendant's negligence, resulting in the plaintiff's injury.

FEDERAL EMPLOYERS' LIABILITY ACT Permits federal employees to file suit for injuries sustained as a result of their employer's negligent conduct.

JUDGMENT N.O.V. A judgment entered by the trial judge reversing a jury verdict if the jury's determination has no basis in law or fact.

International Conflicts

Quick Reference Rules of Law

United States v. Yunis

Government (P) v. Hijacker (D)

681 F. Supp. 896 (D.D.C. 1988).

NATURE OF CASE: Motion to dismiss various indictments in prosecution for hostage taking and airline hijacking.

FACT SUMMARY: Yunis (D) contended that he could not be prosecuted by the Government (P) for a hijacking that he perpetrated when its only connection to the United States was that several Americans were aboard.

🏛 RULE OF LAW
An airline hijacker may be prosecuted by the federal government even if the hijacking's only connection with the United States was the presence of Americans on board.

FACTS: Yunis (D) and several accomplices hijacked a Jordanian airliner while it was on the ground in Beirut. It flew to several locations around the Mediterranean Sea, and eventually flew back to Beirut, where the hijackers blew up the plane and then escaped into the hills. The only connection between the entire episode and the United States was that several Americans were on board the whole time. Yunis (D) was indicted for violating the Hostage Taking Act, 18 U.S.C. § 1203. He was apprehended, and later indicted under the Destruction of Aircraft Act, 18 U.S.C. § 32. He moved to dismiss on jurisdictional grounds.

ISSUE: May an airline hijacker be prosecuted by the federal government even if the hijacking's only connection with the United States was that several Americans were aboard?

HOLDING AND DECISION: (Parker, J.) Yes. An airline hijacker may be prosecuted by the federal government even if the hijacking's only connection with the United States was that several Americans were aboard. For jurisdiction in such a situation to exist, there must be jurisdiction under both international and domestic law. International law relates to the power of Congress to have extraterritorial application of its law; domestic law relates to its intent to do so. International law recognizes several bases for a nation to give extraterritorial application to its laws. One is the "universal principle." Some acts are considered to be so heinous and contrary to civilization that any court may assert jurisdiction. What acts fall within this category are largely defined by international convention. Numerous conventions condemn hijacking and hostage taking, so the universal principle applies. Also relevant is the "passive personal principle," which applies to offenses against a nation's citizens abroad. While the United States has been slow to recognize this principle, it is now generally agreed upon. International law having been disposed of on this issue, domestic law must now be discussed. The Hostage Taking Act, at subsection (b)(1)(A), clearly includes an offender that has seized or detained a U.S. citizen. The language could not be plainer. As to the Destruction of Aircraft Act, it appears from the language of the Act and the Federal Aviation Act, 18 U.S.C. § 31, that the law was intended to apply only when the aircraft in question either began or ended its flight in the United States. Since the flight in question did not do this, the Act does not apply. Motion denied in part; granted in part.

⏵ ANALYSIS

Three other generally accepted bases for jurisdiction exist. These are territorial (jurisdiction over territory), national (jurisdiction over a person) and protective (jurisdiction necessary to protect a state.) Of the five generally recognized jurisdictional grounds, the passive personal principle has been the one to meet with the most resistance by U.S. courts and officials.

Quicknotes

MOTION TO DISMISS Motion to terminate an action based on the adequacy of the pleadings, improper service or venue, etc.

Equal Employment Opportunity Commission v. Arabian American Oil Co.

Employee (P) v. Employer (D)

499 U.S. 244 (1991).

NATURE OF CASE: Review of order dismissing civil rights action for damages for employment discrimination.

FACT SUMMARY: Boureslan (P), an American working abroad for Aramco (D), an American corporation, claimed employment discrimination in violation of the 1964 Civil Rights Act.

RULE OF LAW
The 1964 Civil Rights Act does not apply to American employers abroad.

FACTS: Boureslan (P) had been an employee of Arabian American Oil Co. (Aramco) (D), working in Saudi Arabia. He was discharged, and thereafter filed a suit in U.S. District Court, claiming employment discrimination on the basis of race, religion, and national origin, in violation of the 1964 Civil Rights Act. The district court dismissed, ruling that the Act had no extraterritorial application. The Fifth Circuit affirmed, and the Supreme Court granted review.

ISSUE: Does the 1964 Civil Rights Act apply to American employers abroad?

HOLDING AND DECISION: (Rehnquist, C.J.) No. The 1964 Civil Rights Act does not apply to American employers abroad. The sole determination to make in this issue is the intent of Congress. The analysis begins with the presumption that laws are not intended to have extraterritorial application. To reach a contrary conclusion, a court must find clear evidence of legislative intent. The Act contains no language to this effect. The jurisdictional language in the statute, while broad, is ambiguous as to extraterritorial application. Further, the Act provides no mechanisms for foreign enforcements and contains no provisions for conflicts with foreign laws, as most statutes with foreign application do. Here, the Equal Employment Opportunity Commission (P), which has intervened, urges extraterritorial application. Courts must show some deference to administrative agency interpretations of law, but the final decision must be left to the courts. Here, it seems clear that Congress did not intend the Act to have foreign application. Affirmed.

ANALYSIS

The presumption against extraterritorial application of a law is just that, a presumption. It does not address the power of Congress to legislate in such a manner. This power, without doubt, exists. It is universally recognized in international law that a government can legislate regarding the activities of its citizens abroad.

Quicknotes

CIVIL RIGHTS ACT OF 1964—Title VII Prohibits employment and discrimination based on race, color, religion, sex or national origin.

EEOC Equal Employment Opportunity Commission; an agency created by Title VII to institute nondiscriminatory employment practices pursuant to that statute.

SUBJECT MATTER JURISDICTION The authority of the court to hear and decide actions involving a particular type of issue or subject.

F. Hoffman-La Roche Ltd. v. Empagran S.A.

Vitamin Manufacturers (D) v. Foreign Vitamin Purchasers (P)

542 U.S. 155 (2004).

NATURE OF CASE: Appeal from the D.C. Circuit Court of Appeals in favor of plaintiffs.

FACT SUMMARY: Foreign and domestic purchasers of vitamins brought suit under the Sherman Act alleging that the defendants, foreign and domestic manufacturers of vitamins, had allegedly conspired to fix prices, raising prices in the United States and to foreign customers.

> 🏛 **RULE OF LAW**
> The Foreign Trade Antitrust Improvements Act of 1982 (FTAIA) excludes from the Sherman Antitrust Act claims arising out of foreign injury that are entirely independent of the domestic effects of the allegedly anticompetitive conduct.

FACTS: Plaintiffs, foreign and domestic purchasers of vitamins (P), brought suit against manufacturers (D) of vitamins alleging that the manufacturers engaged in a price fixing scheme in violation of the Sherman Act. The manufacturers (D) moved to dismiss the foreign purchasers, who hailed from Ecuador, Ukraine, Panama, and Australia. The District Court allowed the motion on the grounds that the FTAIA excludes from the Sherman Act anticompetitive conduct that only causes foreign injuries. There is no dispute that the relevant transactions involving the foreign purchasers all occurred outside of United States commerce. The appeals court reversed, holding that the FTAIA's domestic injury exception applied here. Under that exception, the Sherman Act will apply where the price fixing conspiracy had a direct effect on domestic trade and commerce and such effect gave rise to a Sherman Act claim. The manufacturers (D) appealed.

ISSUE: Does the Foreign Trade Antitrust Improvements Act of 1982 (FTAIA) exclude from the Sherman Antitrust Act claims arising out of foreign injury that are entirely independent of the domestic effects of the allegedly anticompetitive conduct?

HOLDING AND DECISION: (Breyer, J.) Yes. The Foreign Trade Antitrust Improvements Act of 1982 (FTAIA) excludes from the Sherman Antitrust Act claims arising out of foreign injury that are entirely independent of the domestic effects of the allegedly anticompetitive conduct. The domestic plaintiffs are not part of this appeal. Regarding the foreign plaintiffs, where their claim is based on the independent foreign effect of the price fixing scheme, they have no claim under the Sherman Act. The purpose of the FTAIA was to inform American exporters that the Sherman Act does not prevent them from engaging in business practices that may be anti-competitive as long as those practices only affect foreign markets. There is an exception for conduct that both (1) has a direct, substantial and reasonably foreseeable effect on American commerce and (2) has an effect of a kind the Sherman Act considers unlawful. The crux of this case is that while the price fixing scheme may have a domestic effect, the foreign plaintiffs' claims arise only from the independent foreign effects of the scheme. Hence, the FTAIA exception will not apply. Because of principles of comity between nations, our nation's antitrust laws should not apply to conduct causing foreign harm. Doing so would interfere with another nation's ability to regulate its own commercial industries. Moreover, applying our antitrust laws in this case would give incentive for foreign plaintiffs to use this nation's courts and treble damages laws to obtain favorable rulings. Congress created the FTAIA to limit and not to expand the scope of the Sherman Act. Again, our holding is limited to those claims that arise solely from independently caused foreign injuries. Lastly, we have assumed here that the domestic effects of the pricing scheme did not relate or give rise to the foreign plaintiffs' claims. The foreign plaintiffs contend the higher prices in the United States allowed the manufacturers to maintain their international price-fixing scheme and thus gave rise to the foreign injury. The Court of Appeals did not address this issue. The Court will thus remand the case for a determination whether the issue was properly preserved and, if so, whether there is a related domestic effect giving rise to the foreign plaintiffs' claims. Reversed and remanded.

CONCURRENCE: (Scalia, J.) The court's interpretation of FTAIA is correct. Statutes should be read with deference to other countries' desire to apply their own laws to conduct within their own territories.

📌 **ANALYSIS**

On remand, the D.C. Court of Appeals found the maintenance of high prices in the United States did not give rise to the injuries alleged by the foreign plaintiffs. The significance of this 8-0 decision (Justice O'Conner recused herself) was the Court's reliance on comity among nations to support its decision.

Quicknotes

SHERMAN ACT Prohibits unreasonable restraint of trade.

SHERMAN ACT § 1 Prohibits price-fixing.

SHERMAN ACT § 2 Makes it a felony to monopolize or attempt to monopolize, or combine or conspire with any other person(s) to monopolize, any part of the trade or commerce among the states or with a foreign country.

United States v. Verdugo-Urquidez

Employees (P) v. Employer (D)

494 U.S. 259 (1990).

NATURE OF CASE: Review of order suppressing evidence in narcotics investigation of a foreign national.

FACT SUMMARY: The Government (P), prosecuting Verdugo-Urquidez (D), a Mexican, for narcotics violations, alleged that the Fourth Amendment did not apply to foreign nationals arrested outside the United States.

🏛 RULE OF LAW
The Fourth Amendment does not apply to the search and seizure by United States agents of property that is owned by a nonresident alien and located in a foreign country.

FACTS: The Government (P) suspected that Verdugo-Urquidez (D), a Mexican national living in Mexico, was a drug kingpin. At the request of the Drug Enforcement Agency (DEA), Verdugo-Urquidez (D) was arrested and turned over at the border to DEA officials. DEA officials then, with the cooperation of Mexican officials, searched his two residences. Incriminating evidence was found. Indicted on numerous narcotics violation counts, Verdugo-Urquidez (D) moved to suppress. The motion was granted. The Government (P) appealed, contending that the Fourth Amendment did not apply to foreign nationals arrested outside U.S. territory. A divided panel of the Court of Appeals for the Ninth Circuit affirmed. The Supreme Court granted certiorari.

ISSUE: Does the Fourth Amendment apply to the search and seizure by United States agents of property that is owned by a nonresident alien and located in a foreign country?

HOLDING AND DECISION: (Rehnquist, C.J.) No. The Fourth Amendment does not apply to the search and seizure by United States agents of property that is owned by a nonresident alien and located in a foreign country. Any restrictions on overseas searches and seizures must be imposed by the political branches through diplomatic understanding, treaty, or legislation. Reversed.

CONCURRENCE: (Kennedy, J.) The conditions and considerations of this case would make adherence to the Fourth Amendment's warrant requirement impracticable and anomalous.

DISSENT: (Brennan, J.) The court today creates an antilogy: the Constitution authorizes our government to enforce our criminal laws abroad, but when government agents exercise this authority, the Fourth Amendment does not travel with them.

▶ ANALYSIS

The court acknowledged that foreign nationals would be protected by the Fifth Amendment. It tried to distinguish the Fourth Amendment, which applies only to "the people," from the Fifth Amendment, which speaks in the relatively universal term of "person." The dissent disagreed on this point.

Quicknotes

CERTIORARI A discretionary writ issued by a superior court to an inferior court in order to review the lower court's decisions; the Supreme Court's writ ordering such review.

EXCLUSIONARY RULE A rule precluding the introduction at trial of evidence unlawfully obtained in violation of the federal constitutional safeguards against unreasonable searches and seizures.

FIFTH AMENDMENT Provides that no person shall be compelled to serve as a witness against himself, or be subject to trial for the same offense twice, or be deprived of life, liberty, or property without due process of law.

FOURTH AMENDMENT Provides that persons be secure as to their person and private belongings against unreasonable searches and seizures.

Boumediene v. Bush

Detainee (P) v. Federal Government (D)

128 S.Ct. 2229, 553 U.S. 723 (2008).

NATURE OF CASE: Appeal from decision of the D.C. Circuit Court of Appeals in favor of the government.

FACT SUMMARY: Boumediene (P), a detainee at Guantanamo Bay, Cuba, filed a petition for habeas corpus.

RULE OF LAW
Because Guantanamo Bay is under the complete and total control of the United States, the Constitution's writ of habeas corpus has full effect for detainees held on the base.

FACTS: [The text's portion of the opinion does not give a full description of Boumediene's capture and detention. Boumediene was a detainee at Guantanamo Bay.] In *Rasul v. Bush*, 542 U.S. 466 (2004), the Court held Guantanamo Bay detainees could file habeas petitions. In 2006, Congress passed the Military Commissions Act (MCA) in response to *Rasul*. The MCA stripped federal courts of jurisdiction to hear habeas petitions for enemy combatants. The D.C. Circuit Court held the writ did not apply to Guantanamo Bay detainees and that Congress could validly remove federal court jurisdiction for habeas petitions from enemy combatants. Boumediene (P) appealed.

ISSUE: Because Guantanamo Bay is under the complete and total control of the United States, does the Constitution's writ of habeas corpus have full effect for detainees held on the base?

HOLDING AND DECISION: (Kennedy, J.) Yes. Because Guantanamo Bay is under the complete and total control of the United States, the Constitution's writ of habeas corpus has full effect for detainees held on the base. The Constitution's Suspension Clause includes the right to habeas corpus unless the right is suspended in times of rebellion or invasion. The central issue to the case is whether persons detained abroad may file for habeas corpus. There is little precedent on the issue. The government contends that because Cuba retains legal sovereignty over Guantanamo Bay, the detainees are not afforded constitutional protection. However, there is no dispute the United States has complete jurisdiction and control over the base due to its lease with the Cuban government. Clearly, the United States has de facto sovereignty over the territory. In a series of prior decisions known as the Insular Cases, this Court held that in unincorporated territories of the United States, the federal government had an obligation to provide noncitizens certain fundamental rights specified in the Constitution. In *Johnson v. Eisentrager*, 339 U.S. 763 (1950), this Court denied the writ to enemy aliens detained at a prison in Germany during the Allies' postwar occupation of Germany. While the court may have held that the lack of sovereignty over the prison in

Germany was the decisive factor not to grant the writ, that decision did not say the locale of the detention was the only factor. Rather, that decision also applied a functional approach to a determination if the writ should apply. From that decision, the Court presents three factors that shall determine the extent of the Suspension Clause: 1) the citizenship and status of the detainee and the process afforded to the detainee to determine that status; 2) the site of the apprehension and detention; and 3) the practical considerations in bestowing the writ upon the detainee. The procedures offered to detainees via the Combatant Status Review Tribunal are too limited to afford an adequate alternative to a habeas petition. No lawyer is afforded and the government's evidence is offered a presumption of validity. Regarding the locale of the detention, the United States' interest in Guantanamo Bay is not transient like it was in the *Eisentrager* matter. Guantanamo Bay is not abroad—it is within the "constant jurisdiction" of the United States. As to the third factor, the government presents no evidence the military mission will be compromised by allowing detainees to file habeas petitions. Accordingly, the Court holds that the writ of habeas corpus has full effect in Guantanamo Bay. The MCA does not purport to be a formal suspension of the writ, and the government does not argue that it is. Therefore, the MCA is in violation of the Suspension Clause and the Guantanamo Bay detainees have the privilege of filing habeas corpus petitions. Reversed.

DISSENT: (Scalia, J.) For the first time in our country's history, this Court has extended the writ of habeas corpus to alien enemies detained abroad. Guantanamo Bay is within the sovereignty of Cuba. In the *Eisentrager* case, this court held clearly that the writ is not available for enemy combatants who were never held within the territory of the United States. That decision is dispositive here. The majority's extrapolation of a so-called functional test from *Eisentrager* is a pure misreading of the case. The decisive factor in that case, as it should be here, was that the detainees were not held on U.S. soil. Moreover, the majority's statement that it is this Court's duty to say what the law is forgets the fact that this Court is one of limited jurisdiction. Congress has spoken clearly on the issue. Unfortunately, this Court, the least qualified branch of government, now has the responsibility of determining how enemy combatants shall be handled.

ANALYSIS

Note that at the end of the majority opinion, the Court states the MCA did not purport to be a suspension of the writ of habeas on the grounds the nation was in a time of

Continued on next page.

rebellion or invasion. Instead, Congress only removed a class of cases from federal jurisdiction. If Congress sought to actually suspend the writ, it would have to do so expressly. The judicial analysis would then be entirely different. However, because that did not happen, the only question was whether the MCA conflicted with the Suspension Clause. The five justice majority held that it did.

■══■

Quicknotes

SUSPENSION CLAUSE A clause found in Article I of the Constitution that protects against arbitrary suspensions of the writ of habeas corpus.

WRIT OF HABEAS CORPUS A proceeding in which a defendant brings a writ to compel a judicial determination of whether he is lawfully being held in custody.

■══■

W. v. Ms. W.

Husband (P) v. Wife (D)

Amtliche Sammlung der Entscheidungen des schweizerischen
Bundesgerichts (vol.) 118 (1992) II (p.) 79 [Swiss Federal Supreme Court (1992)].

NATURE OF CASE: Appeal from support portion of marital dissolution order.

FACT SUMMARY: In a dissolution action involving U.S. citizens no longer living in the United States, a Swiss court applied local law.

🏛 RULE OF LAW
In a dissolution action involving foreign citizens no longer living in their country of origin, a Swiss court should apply local law.

FACTS: W. (P) was a German national and Ms. W. (D) was a Canadian citizen at the time they married in 1960. They then took up residence in Texas. They became U.S. citizens in 1962. Between 1960 and 1976, due to W.'s (P) military career, the couple lived in various locations around the world. In 1979, they settled in Switzerland. In 1986, W. (P) filed a dissolution action in Switzerland. Ms. W. (D) had left in 1984 and stayed in Germany until 1990, whereupon she returned to Switzerland. While she was still in Germany, a Swiss court, applying local law, entered a divorce decree awarding Ms. W. (D) 1500 francs support per month. W. (P) appealed.

ISSUE: In a dissolution action involving foreign citizens no longer living in their country of origin, should a Swiss court apply local law?

HOLDING AND DECISION: [Judge not stated in casebook excerpt.] Yes. In a dissolution action involving foreign citizens no longer living in their country of origin, a Swiss court should apply local law. As a general rule, when both parties are citizens of a country and only one party lives locally, the local court should apply the law of the country of nationality. However, when it is demonstrable that the otherwise-applicable law has only a slight connection to the action and other law has greater connection, that law should be applied. Here, because of the federal character of the United States, a U.S. citizen is usually a citizen of a state as well. The parties were citizens of Texas but had not lived there for many years. Texas thus had very little connection with the parties. The United States has no federal law regarding alimony. This being so, the court below properly applied local law. Affirmed.

▌ *ANALYSIS*

The U.S. federal system is something of an anomaly among nations. While many nations have political subdivisions, few are sovereign as are American states. The court here

was cognizant of the difference between national and state citizenship and correctly applied the distinction in reaching its decision.

■■■

Quicknotes

DISSOLUTION Annulment or termination of a formal or legal bond, tie or contract.

DOMICILE A person's permanent home or principal establishment to which he has an intention of returning when he is absent therefrom.

■■■

Banco Nacional de Cuba v. Sabbatino

Bank (P) v. Receiver (D)

376 U.S. 398 (1964).

NATURE OF CASE: Action to recover payments owed.

FACT SUMMARY: The Cuban government sought to recover money owed pursuant to a contract for the sale of sugar.

RULE OF LAW
The act-of-state doctrine is applicable even if international law has been violated.

FACTS: In response to a U.S. reduction of Cuba's quota for sugar imports, Cuba nationalized the property of Americans in Cuba, including that belonging to Compania Azucarera Vertientes (CAV), a sugar corporation largely owned by U.S. residents. CAV had contracted to sell the sugar to Farr, Whitlock & Co., a U.S. commodities broker. Farr entered into a second contract to buy sugar from the Cuban government. Farr shipped the sugar and received payment but turned the proceeds over to CAV's receiver Sabbatino (D). Cuba assigned its rights under the contract to Banco Nacional (P), which filed suit. Sabbatino (D) argued that Cuba never had any right to the sugar because the appropriation was in violation of international law. The district court found in favor of Sabbatino (D) and the court of appeals affirmed.

ISSUE: Is the act-of-state doctrine applicable even if international law has been violated?

HOLDING AND DECISION: (Harlan, J.) Yes. The act-of-state doctrine is applicable even if international law has been violated. The classic statement of the doctrine is that the courts of one country shall not pass on the acts of another government performed within its own territory. Here, this Court holds that in the absence of any treaty between the two nations, our courts will not examine the validity of the taking of property by the Cuban government within its own territory. This is true even if international law is violated. The potential adverse consequences of a contrary conclusion are demonstrated by contrasting the practices of the political branch with the limitations of the judicial process in these matters. Expropriations of significance are followed by diplomatic negotiations and sanctions, if necessary. Judicial determinations only occasionally may be enforced since the property at issue is typically in another country. Both the national interest and the furtherance of a rule of law among nations are best served by maintaining the integrity of the doctrine. Accordingly, Cuba's decree may not be challenged in this Court. Reversed and remanded.

▶ ANALYSIS

Note that the Court states that international law does not require the application of the act-of-state doctrine, nor is failure to apply it a breach of international obligation. Moreover, it is not required by the U.S. Constitution, but rather a matter of federal common law.

■■■

Quicknotes

ACT-OF-STATE DOCTRINE Prohibits United States courts from investigating acts of other countries committed within the borders of the other country.

■■■

W.S. Kirkpatrick v. Environmental Tectonics Corp.

U.S. company (D) v. Competitor (P)

493 U.S. 400 (1990).

NATURE OF CASE: Review of reversal of summary judgment dismissing action for damages for R.I.C.O. violations.

FACT SUMMARY: W.S. Kirkpatrick Co. (D) contended that the act-of-state doctrine precluded an action based on alleged acceptance by foreign officials of bribes it had offered.

> ## 🏛 RULE OF LAW
> The act-of-state doctrine does not preclude an action against a U.S. concern based on acceptance of proffered bribes by foreign officials.

FACTS: To secure a Nigerian government contract, W.S. Kirkpatrick Co. (D) offered certain Nigerian officials bribes, which were accepted. Kirkpatrick (D) secured the contract. A federal (U.S.) investigation followed, and Kirkpatrick (D) pleaded guilty to violations of the Federal Foreign Corrupt Practices Act. Environmental Tectonics Corp. (P), an unsuccessful bidder for the Nigerian contract, brought an action against Kirkpatrick (D) seeking damages under the federal Racketeer Influenced and Corrupt Organizations Act (R.I.C.O.). The district court dismissed, holding the action barred by the act-of-state doctrine. The Third Circuit reversed. The Supreme Court granted review.

ISSUE: Does the act-of-state doctrine preclude an action against a U.S. concern based on acceptance of proffered bribes by foreign officials?

HOLDING AND DECISION: (Scalia, J.) No. The act-of-state doctrine does not preclude an action against a U.S. concern based on acceptance of proffered bribes by foreign officials. The doctrine only comes into play when a court, in reaching its decision, would have to declare void the act of a foreign government within its own territory. In an action against a domestic corporation or person based on alleged bribes of foreign officials, it is the act of the domestic entity, not the motivation of the foreign official, that is at issue. No foreign act is declared void when this issue is decided, and merely looking at a foreign official's motive is insufficient to invoke the doctrine. Affirmed.

▶ ANALYSIS

The act-of-state doctrine originally was considered a part of international law. In recent years, courts in the United States have come to focus on it more as a component of separation of powers. The judiciary has come to recognize that it is for the political branches of government to conduct foreign policy, and excessive inquiry by the judiciary into the acts of foreign governments would interfere with this.

◼▬◼

Quicknotes

COMITY A rule pursuant to which courts in one state give deference to the statutes and judicial decisions of another.

RICO Racketeer Influenced and Corrupt Organization laws; federal and state statutes enacted for the purpose of prosecuting organized crime.

SEPARATION OF POWERS The system of checks and balances preventing one branch of government from infringing upon exercising the powers of another branch of government.

◼▬◼

Hilton v. Guyot

U.S. citizen (D) v. French company (P)

159 U.S. 113 (1895).

NATURE OF CASE: Appeal from a finding that a French court judgment was enforceable without retrial on the merits.

FACT SUMMARY: Hilton (P) and Libbey (P) appealed from a federal district court holding that a French court judgment against them for sums allegedly owed to a French firm was enforceable without retrial on the merits.

🏛 RULE OF LAW
No law has any effect, of its own force, beyond the limits of the sovereignty from which its authority is derived.

FACTS: Hilton (P) and Libbey (P), New York citizens trading in Paris, were sued in France by Guyot (D), the administrator of a French firm, for sums allegedly owed to that firm. Hilton (P) and Libbey (P) appeared and litigated the merits in the French proceeding. The French court rendered a judgment against them which was affirmed by a higher court and became final. Guyot (D) then sought to enforce that judgment in federal district court in New York. That court held the judgment enforceable without retrial on the merits. Hilton (P) and Libbey (P) subsequently appealed to the U.S. Supreme Court.

ISSUE: Do laws have any effect, of their own force, beyond the limits of the sovereignty from which their authority is derived?

HOLDING AND DECISION: (Gray, J.) No. No law has any effect, of its own force, beyond the limits of the sovereignty from which its authority is derived. No sovereign is bound, unless by special compact, to execute within his dominions a judgment rendered by the tribunals of another state, and if execution be sought by suit upon the judgment or otherwise, the tribunal in which the suit is brought, or from which execution is sought, is, on principle, at liberty to examine into the merits of such judgment, and to give effect to it or not, as may be found just and equitable. The general comity, utility and convenience of nations have, however, established a usage among most civilized states, by which the final judgments of foreign courts of competent jurisdiction are reciprocally carried into execution, under certain regulations and restrictions, which differ in different countries. Moreover, judgments rendered in France, or in any other foreign country, by the laws of which our own judgments are reviewable upon the merits, are not entitled to full credit and conclusive effect when sued upon in this country, but are prima facie evidence only of the justice of the plaintiffs' claim. Reversed.

DISSENT: (Fuller, C.J.) The doctrine of res judicata applicable to domestic judgments should be applied to foreign judgments as well, and rests on the same general ground of public policy that there should be an end of litigation.

▶ ANALYSIS

The Court's decision in *Hilton v. Guyot* reflects the traditional rule of reciprocity. According to this concept, foreign nation judgments were granted the same or comparable treatment as American judgments were given by the judgment nation. Since the Court in *Hilton* found that French courts would not have enforced or executed a judgment rendered in this country, it thus held that the French judgment at issue should be nonconclusive here.

Quicknotes

COMITY A rule pursuant to which courts in one state give deference to the statutes and judicial decisions of another.

IN PERSONAM An action against a person seeking to impose personal liability.

IN REM An action against property.

RECIPROCITY The condition that a state provides the citizens of another the same rights and benefits of its own citizens in exchange for the same treatment.

RES JUDICATA The rule of law that a final judgment by a court precludes subsequent litigation between the parties regarding the same cause of action.

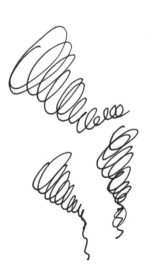

Common Latin Words and Phrases Encountered in the Law

A FORTIORI: Because one fact exists or has been proven, therefore a second fact that is related to the first fact must also exist.

A PRIORI: From the cause to the effect. A term of logic used to denote that when one generally accepted truth is shown to be a cause, another particular effect must necessarily follow.

AB INITIO: From the beginning; a condition which has existed throughout, as in a marriage which was void ab initio.

ACTUS REUS: The wrongful act; in criminal law, such action sufficient to trigger criminal liability.

AD VALOREM: According to value; an ad valorem tax is imposed upon an item located within the taxing jurisdiction calculated by the value of such item.

AMICUS CURIAE: Friend of the court. Its most common usage takes the form of an amicus curiae brief, filed by a person who is not a party to an action but is nonetheless allowed to offer an argument supporting his legal interests.

ARGUENDO: In arguing. A statement, possibly hypothetical, made for the purpose of argument, is one made arguendo.

BILL QUIA TIMET: A bill to quiet title (establish ownership) to real property.

BONA FIDE: True, honest, or genuine. May refer to a person's legal position based on good faith or lacking notice of fraud (such as a bona fide purchaser for value) or to the authenticity of a particular document (such as a bona fide last will and testament).

CAUSA MORTIS: With approaching death in mind. A gift causa mortis is a gift given by a party who feels certain that death is imminent.

CAVEAT EMPTOR: Let the buyer beware. This maxim is reflected in the rule of law that a buyer purchases at his own risk because it is his responsibility to examine, judge, test, and otherwise inspect what he is buying.

CERTIORARI: A writ of review. Petitions for review of a case by the United States Supreme Court are most often done by means of a writ of certiorari.

CONTRA: On the other hand. Opposite. Contrary to.

CORAM NOBIS: Before us; writs of error directed to the court that originally rendered the judgment.

CORAM VOBIS: Before you; writs of error directed by an appellate court to a lower court to correct a factual error.

CORPUS DELICTI: The body of the crime; the requisite elements of a crime amounting to objective proof that a crime has been committed.

CUM TESTAMENTO ANNEXO, ADMINISTRATOR (ADMINISTRATOR C.T.A.): With will annexed; an administrator c.t.a. settles an estate pursuant to a will in which he is not appointed.

DE BONIS NON, ADMINISTRATOR (ADMINISTRATOR D.B.N.): Of goods not administered; an administrator d.b.n. settles a partially settled estate.

DE FACTO: In fact; in reality; actually. Existing in fact but not officially approved or engendered.

DE JURE: By right; lawful. Describes a condition that is legitimate "as a matter of law," in contrast to the term "de facto," which connotes something existing in fact but not legally sanctioned or authorized. For example, de facto segregation refers to segregation brought about by housing patterns, etc., whereas de jure segregation refers to segregation created by law.

DE MINIMIS: Of minimal importance; insignificant; a trifle; not worth bothering about.

DE NOVO: Anew; a second time; afresh. A trial de novo is a new trial held at the appellate level as if the case originated there and the trial at a lower level had not taken place.

DICTA: Generally used as an abbreviated form of obiter dicta, a term describing those portions of a judicial opinion incidental or not necessary to resolution of the specific question before the court. Such nonessential statements and remarks are not considered to be binding precedent.

DUCES TECUM: Refers to a particular type of writ or subpoena requesting a party or organization to produce certain documents in their possession.

EN BANC: Full bench. Where a court sits with all justices present rather than the usual quorum.

EX PARTE: For one side or one party only. An ex parte proceeding is one undertaken for the benefit of only one party, without notice to, or an appearance by, an adverse party.

EX POST FACTO: After the fact. An ex post facto law is a law that retroactively changes the consequences of a prior act.

EX REL.: Abbreviated form of the term "ex relatione," meaning upon relation or information. When the state brings an action in which it has no interest against an individual at the instigation of one who has a private interest in the matter.

FORUM NON CONVENIENS: Inconvenient forum. Although a court may have jurisdiction over the case, the action should be tried in a more conveniently located court, one to which parties and witnesses may more easily travel, for example.

GUARDIAN AD LITEM: A guardian of an infant as to litigation, appointed to represent the infant and pursue his/her rights.

HABEAS CORPUS: You have the body. The modern writ of habeas corpus is a writ directing that a person (body) being detained (such as a prisoner) be brought before the court so that the legality of his detention can be judicially ascertained.

IN CAMERA: In private, in chambers. When a hearing is held before a judge in his chambers or when all spectators are excluded from the courtroom.

IN FORMA PAUPERIS: In the manner of a pauper. A party who proceeds in forma pauperis because of his poverty is one who is allowed to bring suit without liability for costs.

INFRA: Below, under. A word referring the reader to a later part of a book. (The opposite of supra.)

IN LOCO PARENTIS: In the place of a parent.

IN PARI DELICTO: Equally wrong; a court of equity will not grant requested relief to an applicant who is in pari delicto, or as much at fault in the transactions giving rise to the controversy as is the opponent of the applicant.

IN PARI MATERIA: On like subject matter or upon the same matter. Statutes relating to the same person or things are said to be in pari materia. It is a general rule of statutory construction that such statutes should be construed together, i.e., looked at as if they together constituted one law.

IN PERSONAM: Against the person. Jurisdiction over the person of an individual.

IN RE: In the matter of. Used to designate a proceeding involving an estate or other property.

IN REM: A term that signifies an action against the res, or thing. An action in rem is basically one that is taken directly against property, as distinguished from an action in personam, i.e., against the person.

INTER ALIA: Among other things. Used to show that the whole of a statement, pleading, list, statute, etc., has not been set forth in its entirety.

INTER PARTES: Between the parties. May refer to contracts, conveyances or other transactions having legal significance.

INTER VIVOS: Between the living. An inter vivos gift is a gift made by a living grantor, as distinguished from bequests contained in a will, which pass upon the death of the testator.

IPSO FACTO: By the mere fact itself.

JUS: Law or the entire body of law.

LEX LOCI: The law of the place; the notion that the rights of parties to a legal proceeding are governed by the law of the place where those rights arose.

MALUM IN SE: Evil or wrong in and of itself; inherently wrong. This term describes an act that is wrong by its very nature, as opposed to one which would not be wrong but for the fact that there is a specific legal prohibition against it (malum prohibitum).

MALUM PROHIBITUM: Wrong because prohibited, but not inherently evil. Used to describe something that is wrong because it is expressly forbidden by law but that is not in and of itself evil, e.g., speeding.

MANDAMUS: We command. A writ directing an official to take a certain action.

MENS REA: A guilty mind; a criminal intent. A term used to signify the mental state that accompanies a crime or other prohibited act. Some crimes require only a general mens rea (general intent to do the prohibited act), but others, like assault with intent to murder, require the existence of a specific mens rea.

MODUS OPERANDI: Method of operating; generally refers to the manner or style of a criminal in committing crimes, admissible in appropriate cases as evidence of the identity of a defendant.

NEXUS: A connection to.

NISI PRIUS: A court of first impression. A nisi prius court is one where issues of fact are tried before a judge or jury.

N.O.V. (NON OBSTANTE VEREDICTO): Notwithstanding the verdict. A judgment n.o.v. is a judgment given in favor of one party despite the fact that a verdict was returned in favor of the other party, the justification being that the verdict either had no reasonable support in fact or was contrary to law.

NUNC PRO TUNC: Now for then. This phrase refers to actions that may be taken and will then have full retroactive effect.

PENDENTE LITE: Pending the suit; pending litigation under way.

PER CAPITA: By head; beneficiaries of an estate, if they take in equal shares, take per capita.

PER CURIAM: By the court; signifies an opinion ostensibly written "by the whole court" and with no identified author.

PER SE: By itself, in itself; inherently.

PER STIRPES: By representation. Used primarily in the law of wills to describe the method of distribution where a person, generally because of death, is unable to take that which is left to him by the will of another, and therefore his heirs divide such property between them rather than take under the will individually.

PRIMA FACIE: On its face, at first sight. A prima facie case is one that is sufficient on its face, meaning that the evidence supporting it is adequate to establish the case until contradicted or overcome by other evidence.

PRO TANTO: For so much; as far as it goes. Often used in eminent domain cases when a property owner receives partial payment for his land without prejudice to his right to bring suit for the full amount he claims his land to be worth.

QUANTUM MERUIT: As much as he deserves. Refers to recovery based on the doctrine of unjust enrichment in those cases in which a party has rendered valuable services or furnished materials that were accepted and enjoyed by another under circumstances that would reasonably notify the recipient that the rendering party expected to be paid. In essence, the law implies a contract to pay the reasonable value of the services or materials furnished.

QUASI: Almost like; as if; nearly. This term is essentially used to signify that one subject or thing is almost